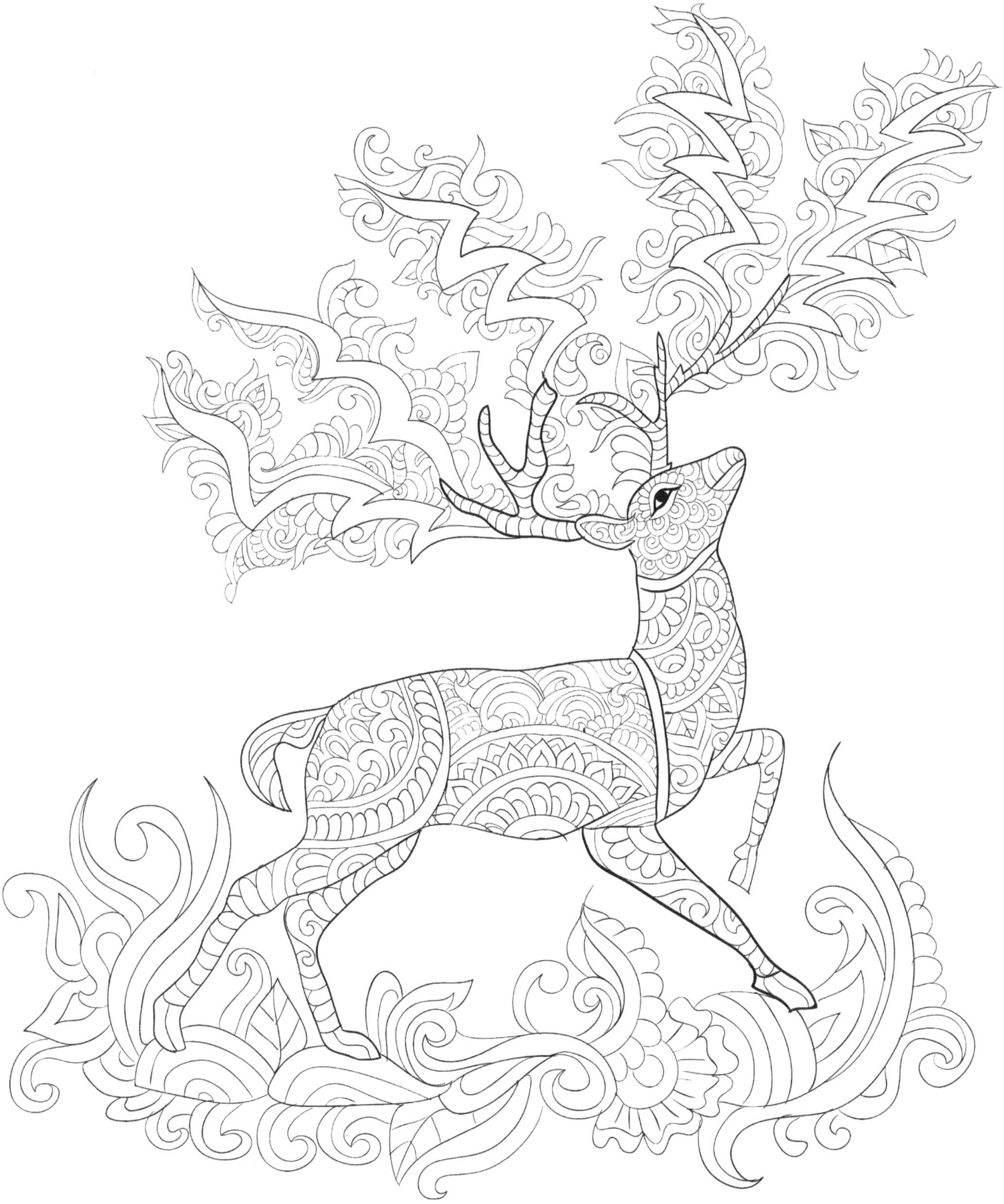

Wherever you go, no matter what the weather, always bring your own sunshine.

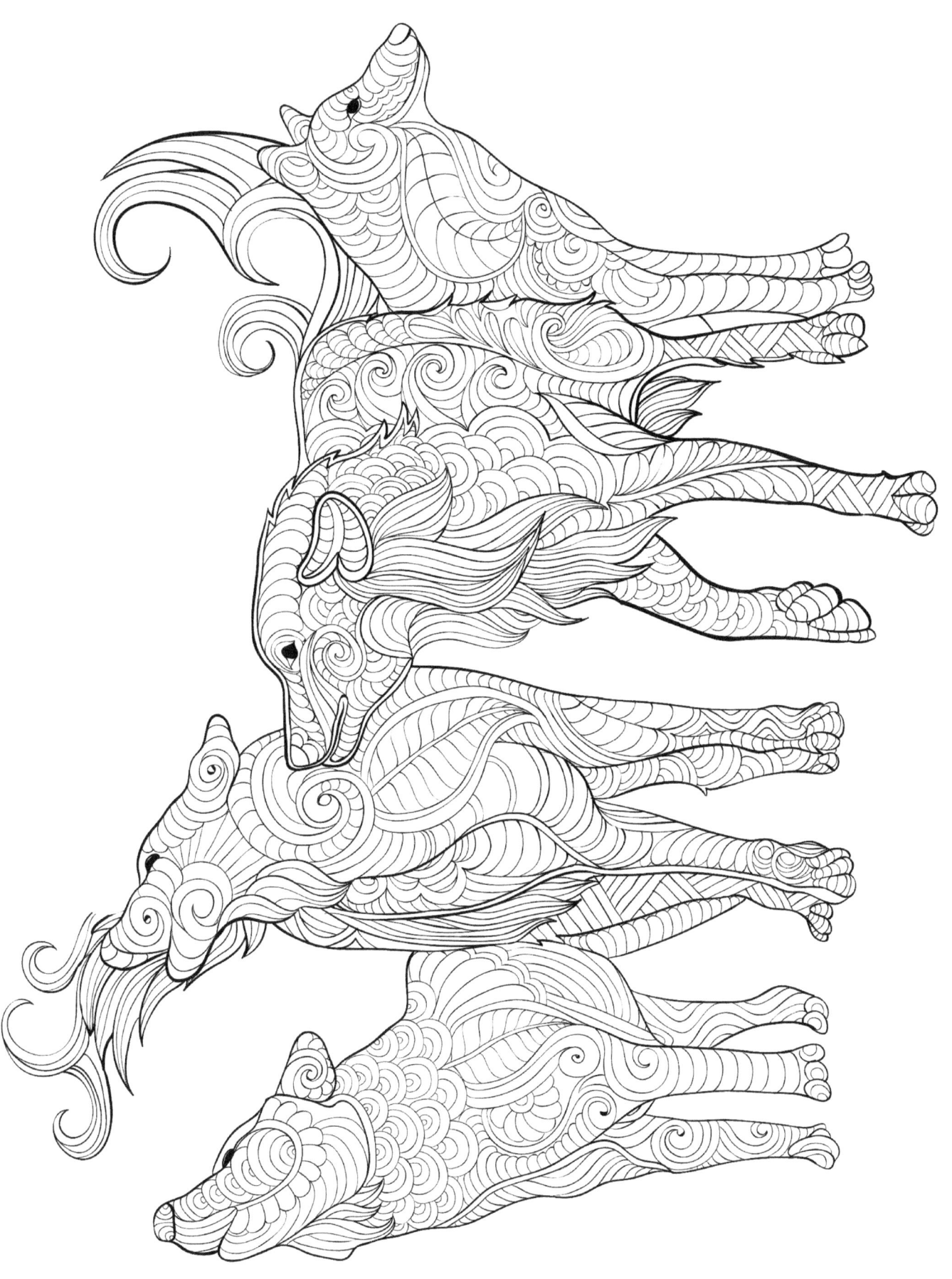

Look deep into nature, and then you will understand everything better.

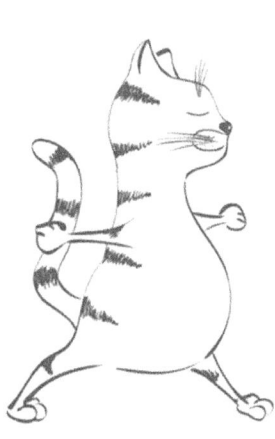
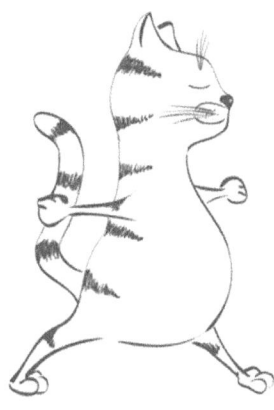
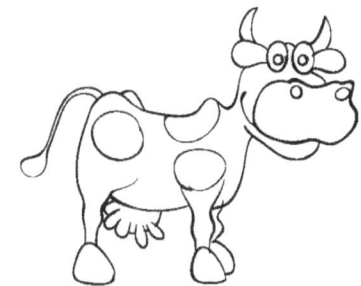
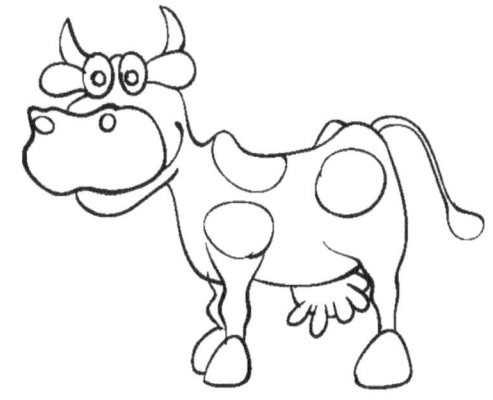

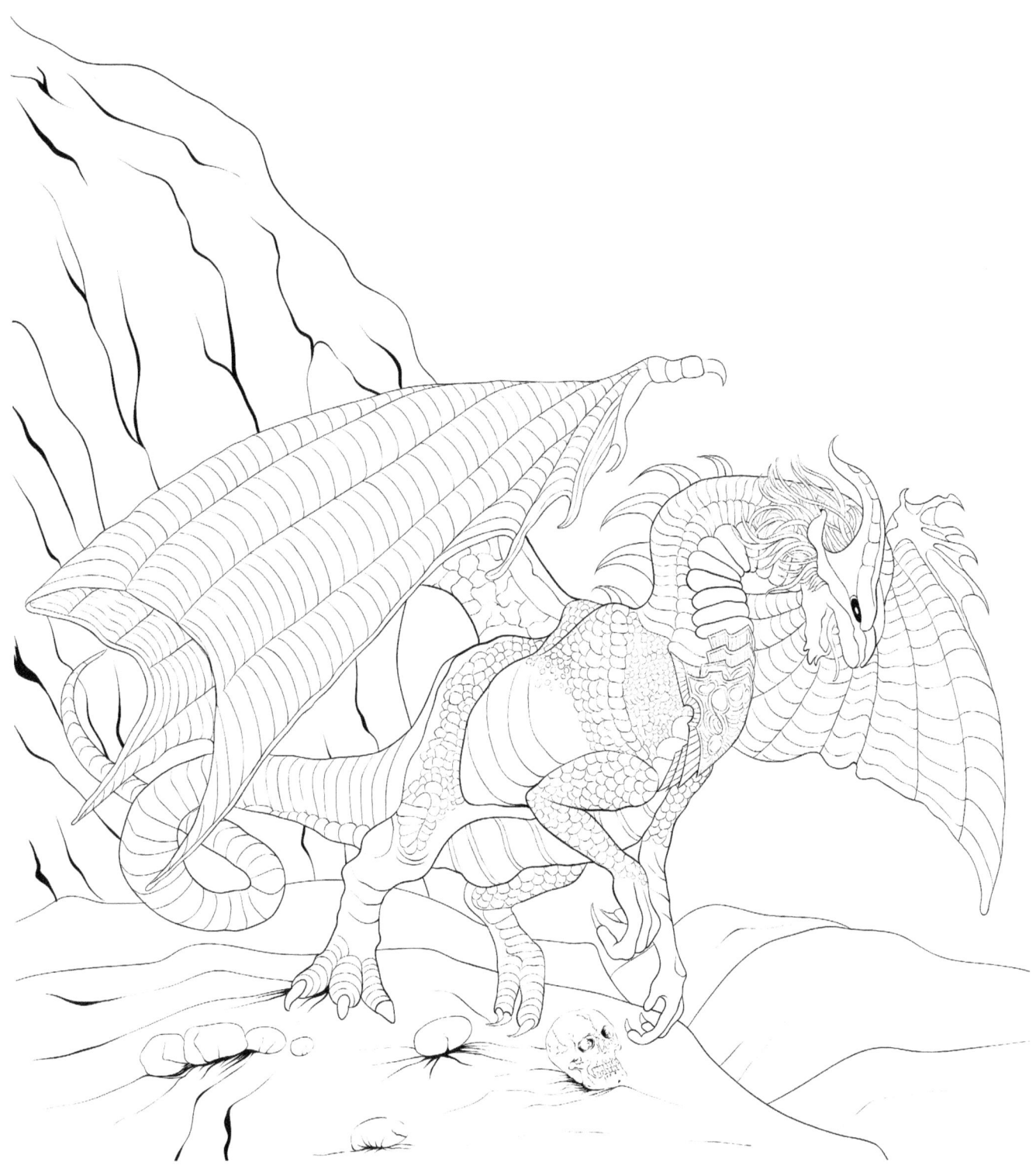

Just living is not enough... one must have sunshine, freedom, and a little flower.

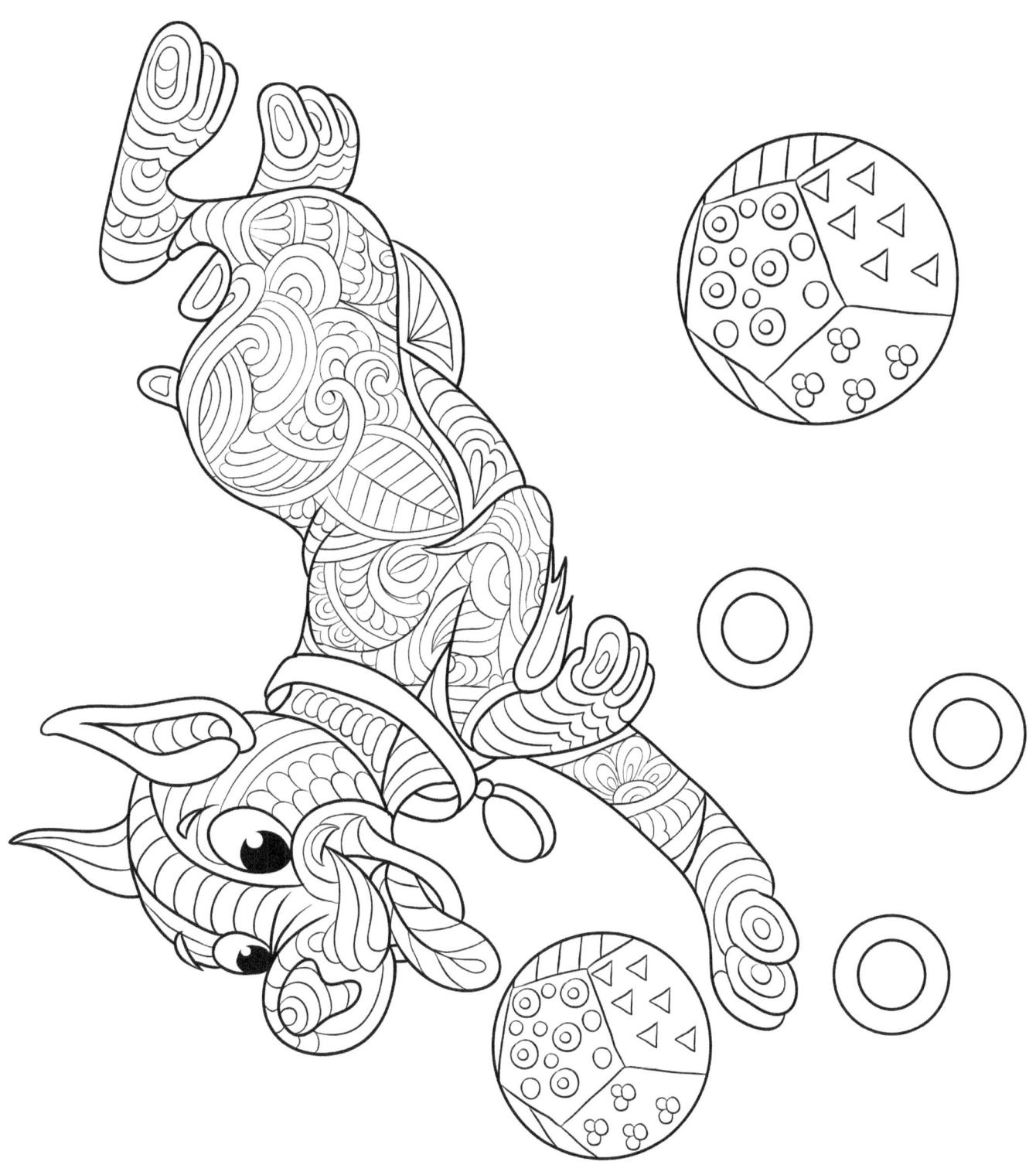

NATURE ALWAYS WEARS THE COLORS OF THE SPIRIT

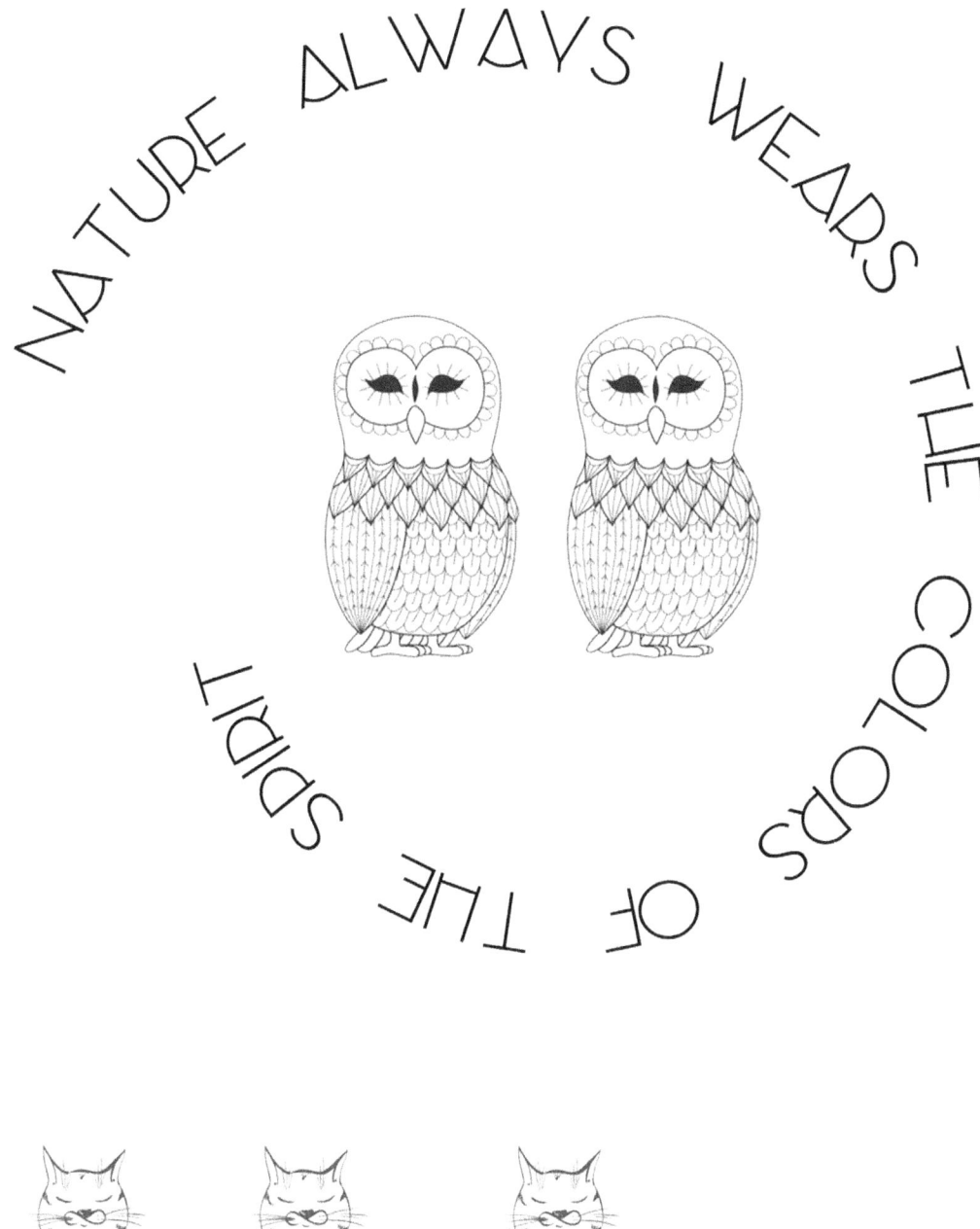

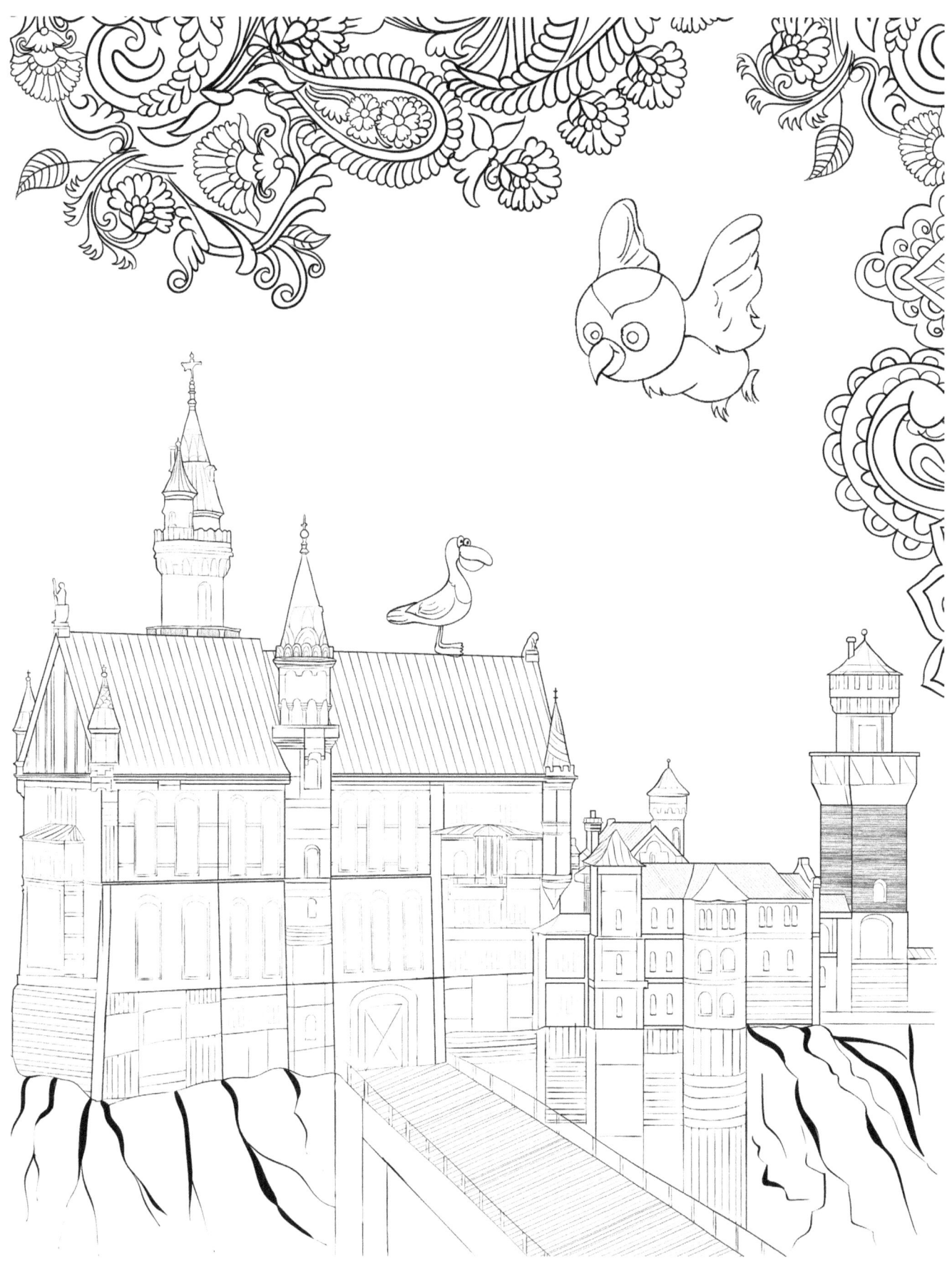

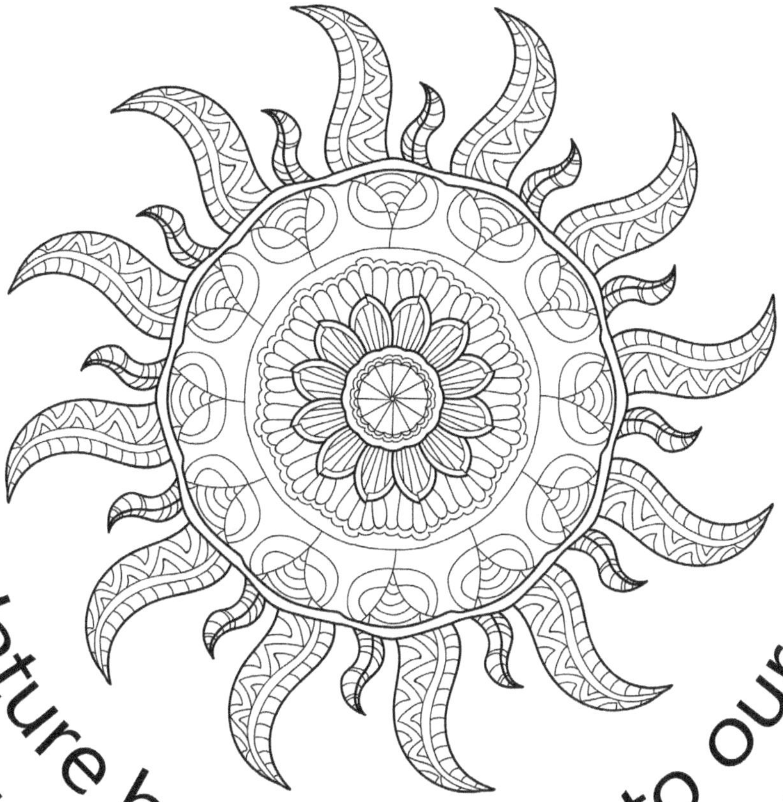

Nature holds the key to our aesthetic, intellectual, cognitive and even spiritual satisfaction.

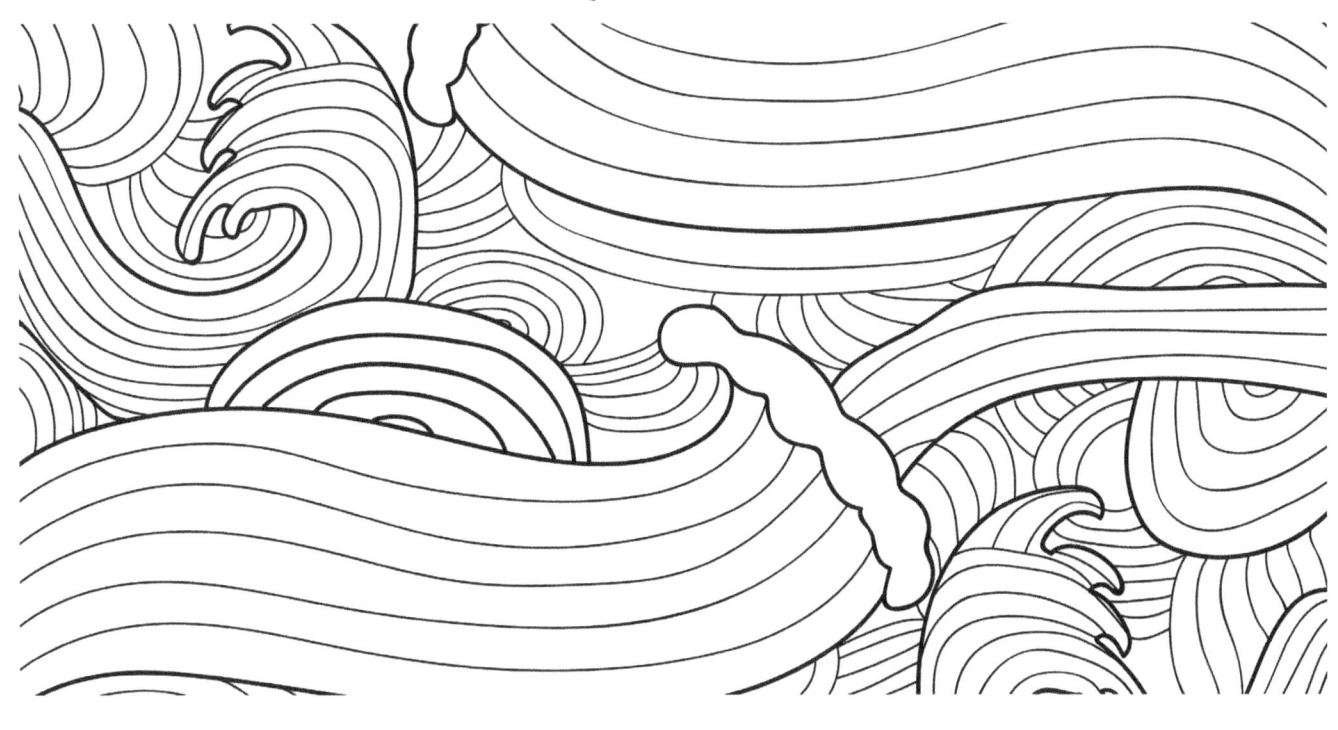

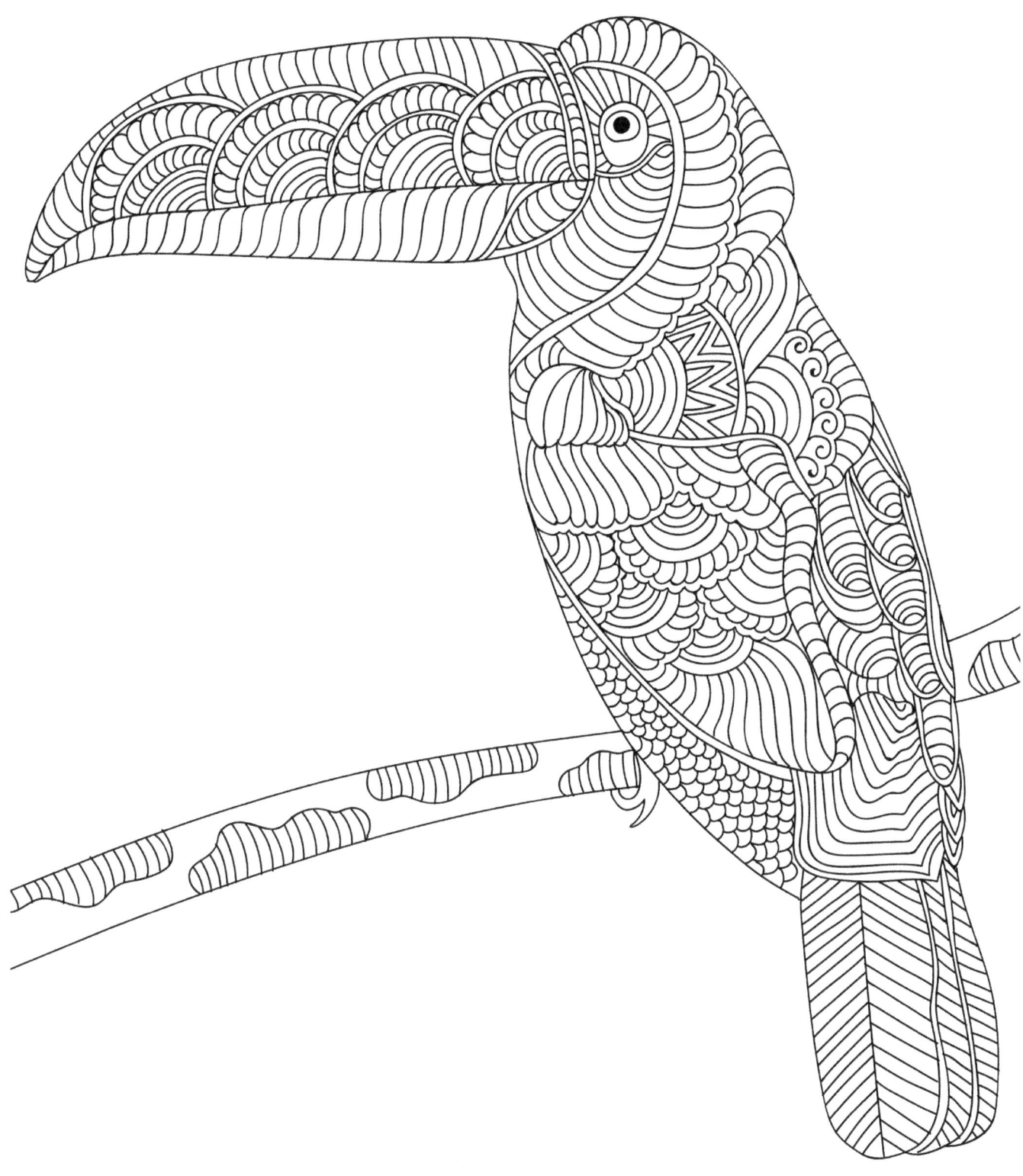

The clearest way into the Universe is through a forest wilderness.

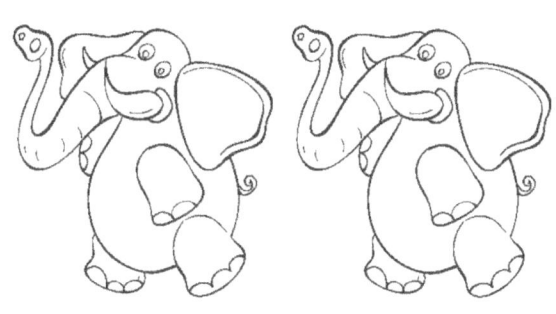

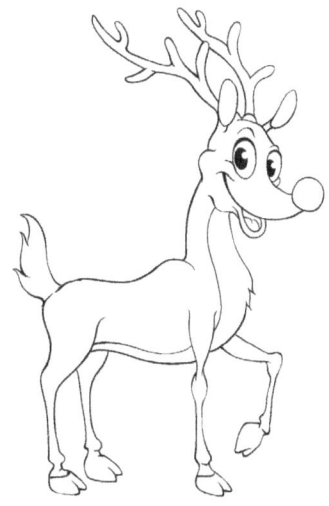

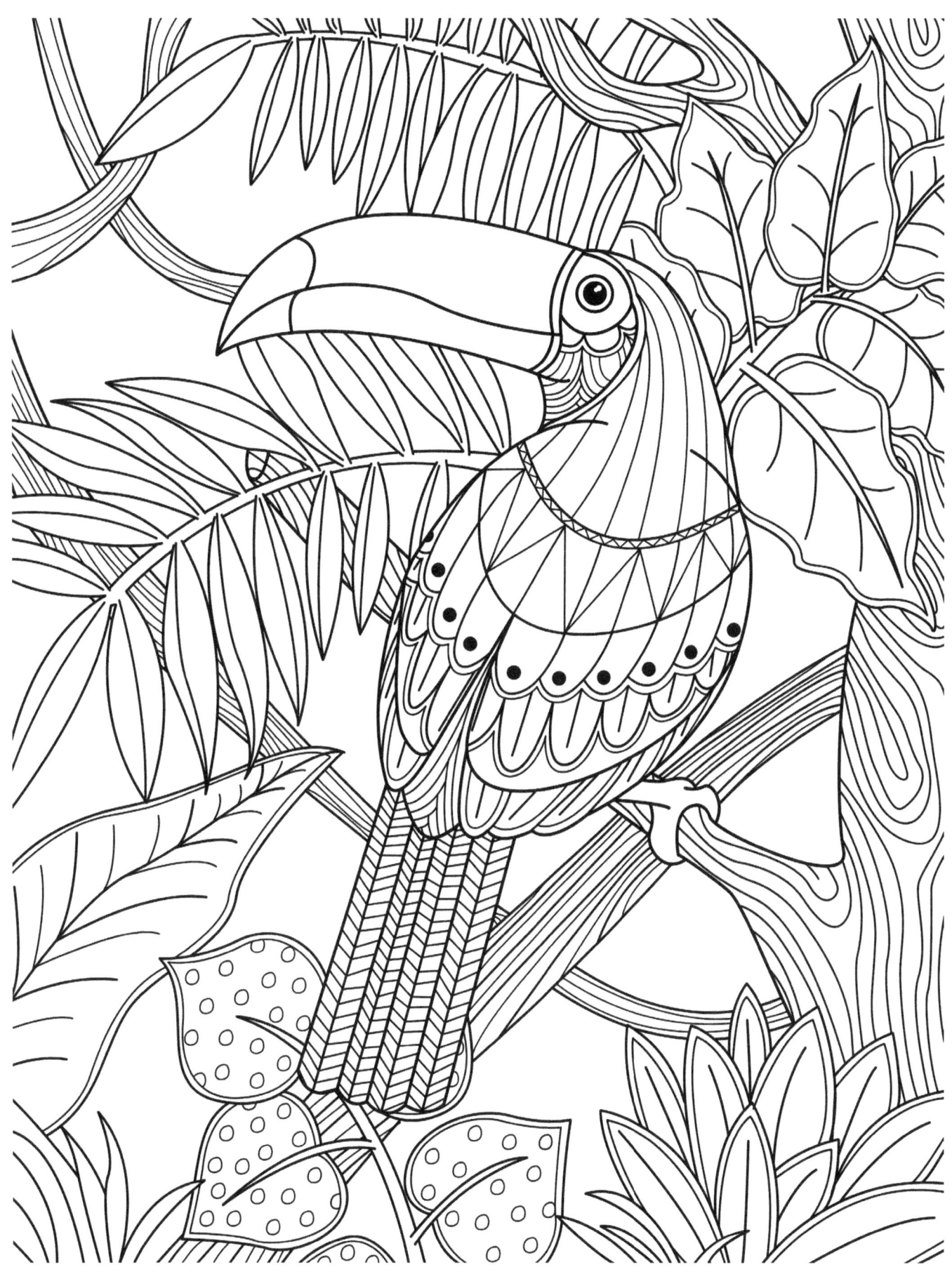

Ocean is more ancient than the mountains, and freighted with the memories and the dreams of Time.

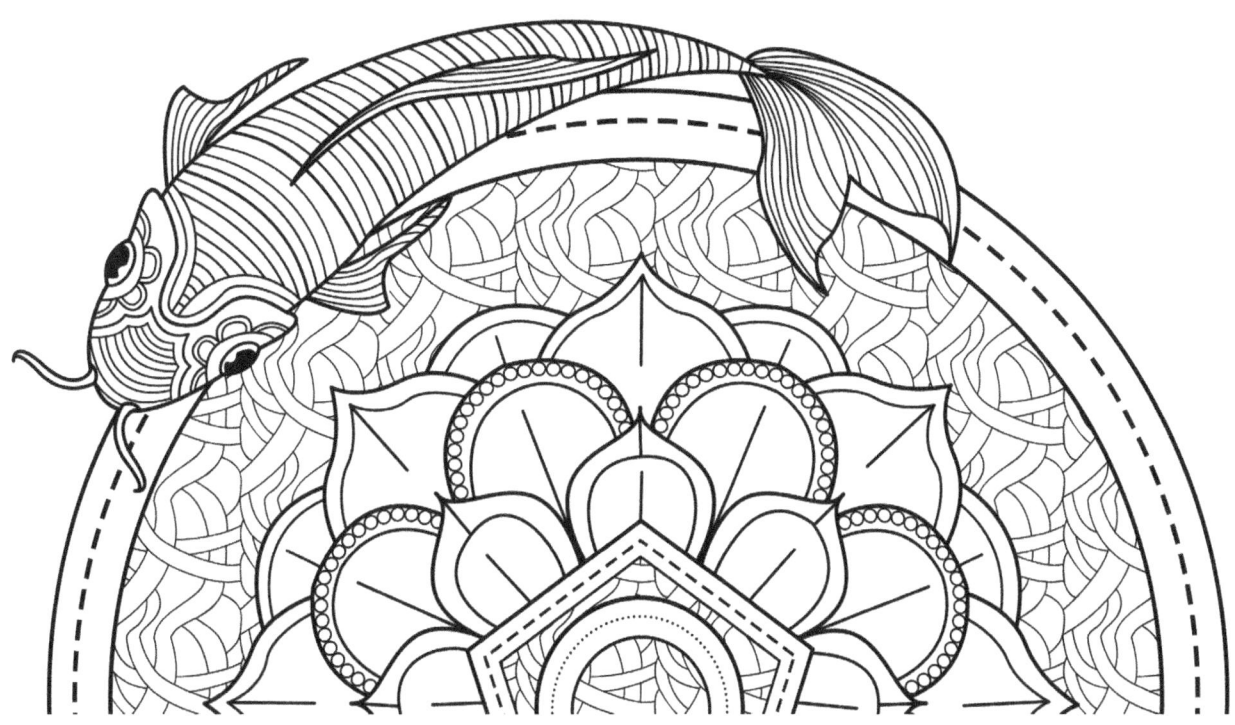

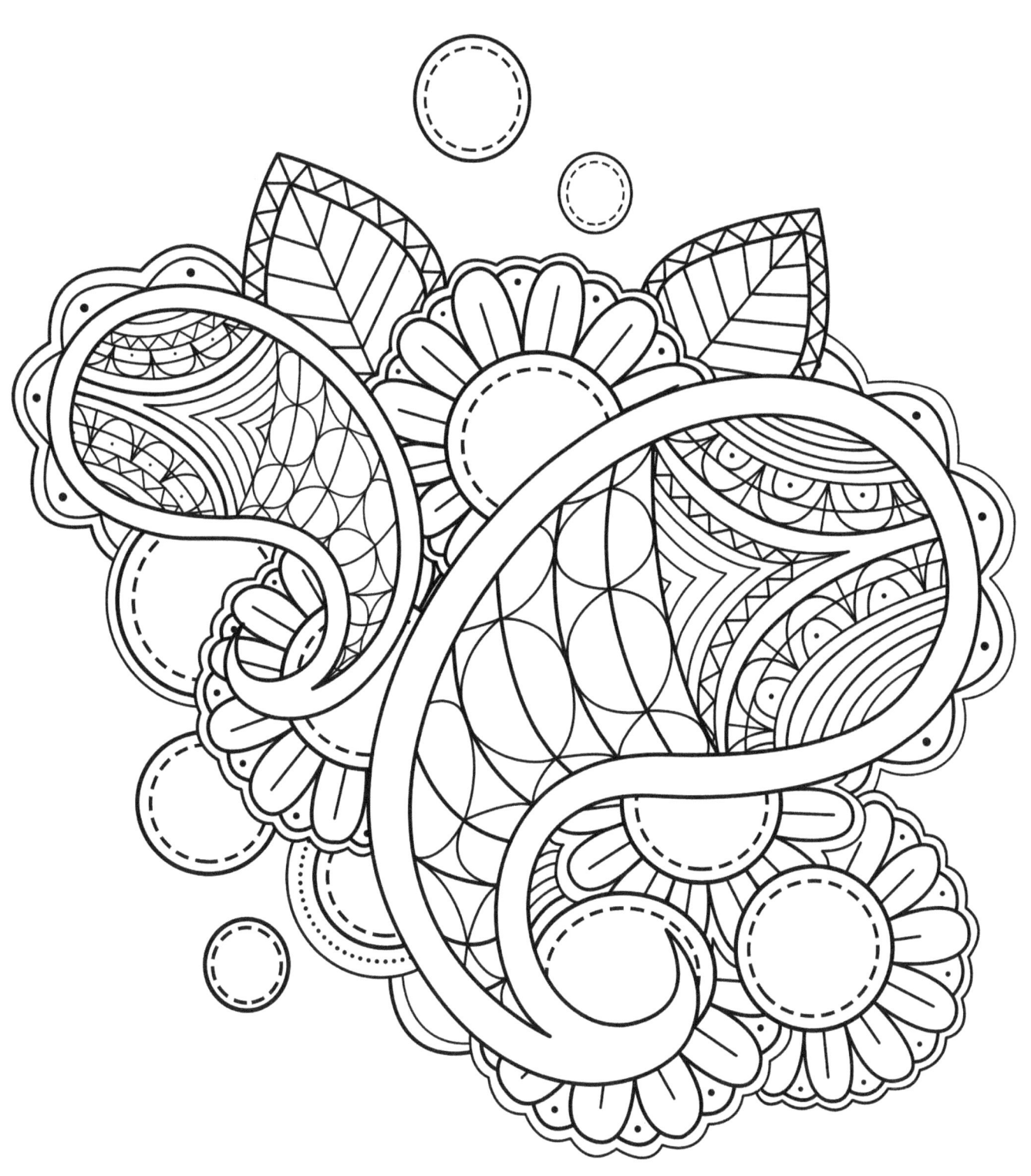

On earth there is no heaven, but there are pieces of it.

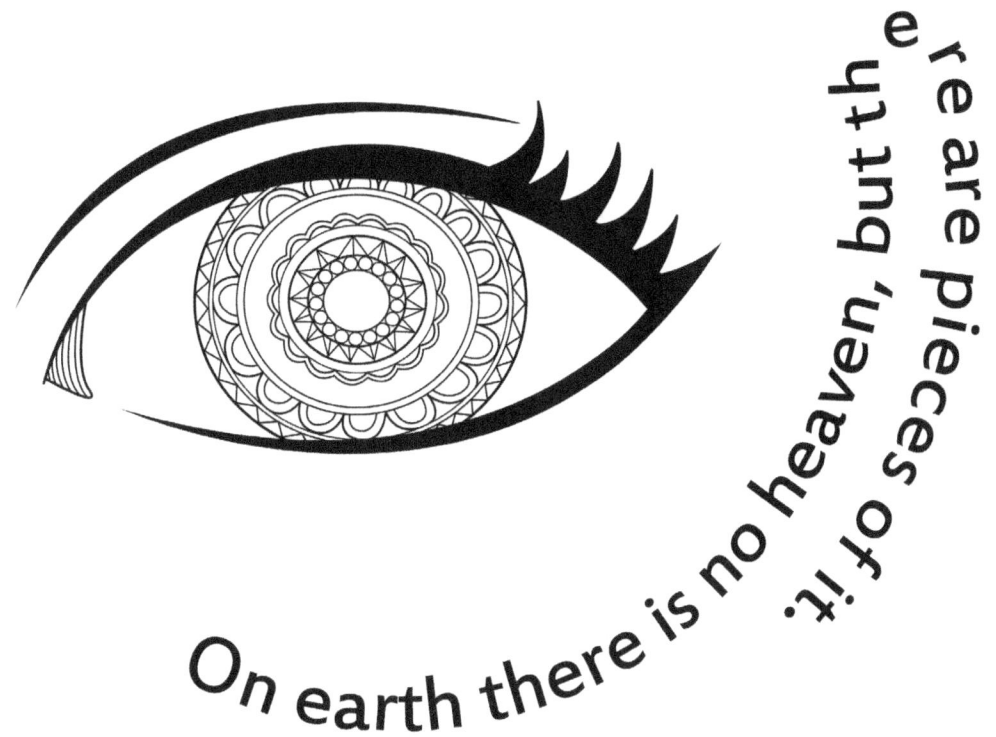

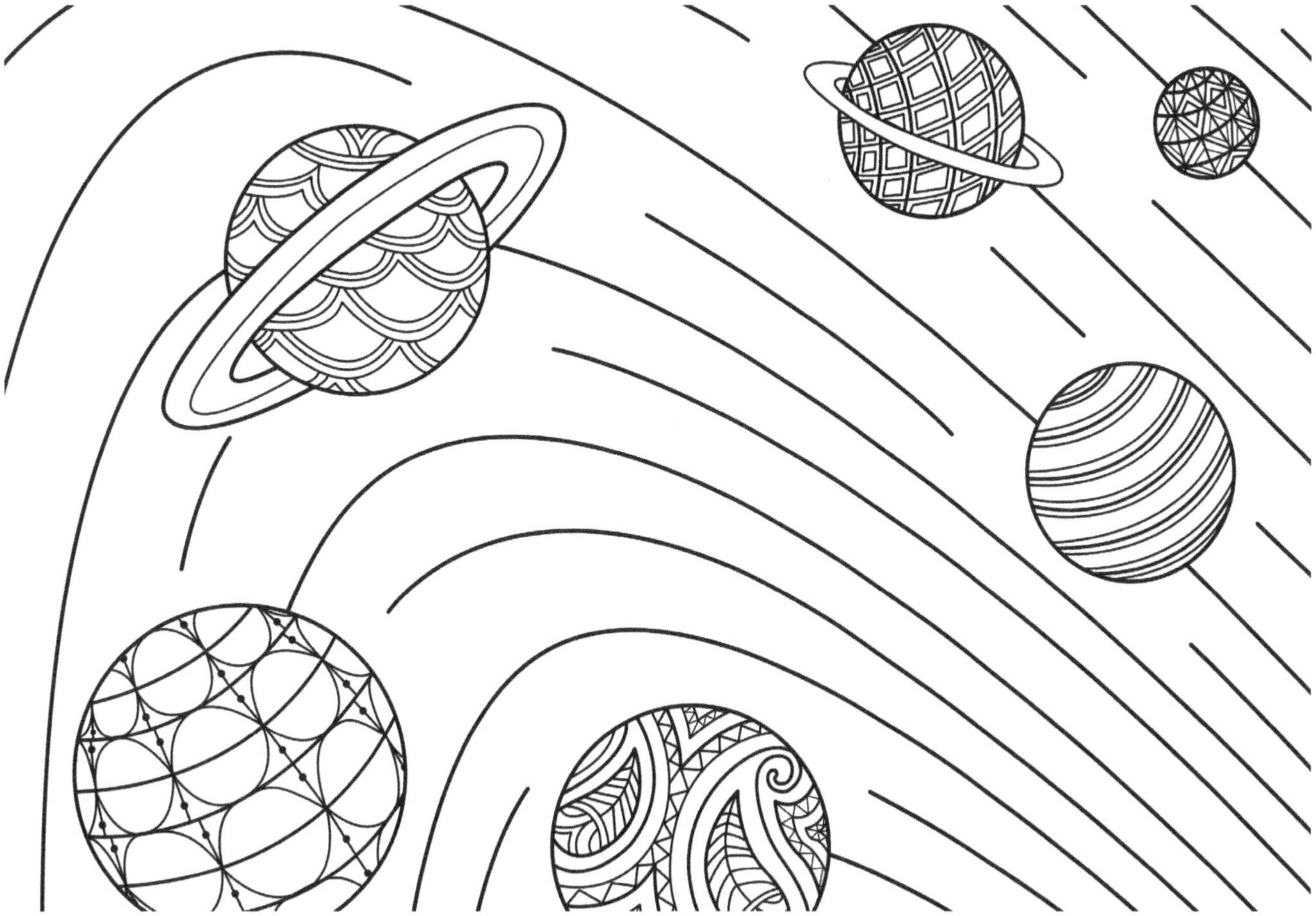

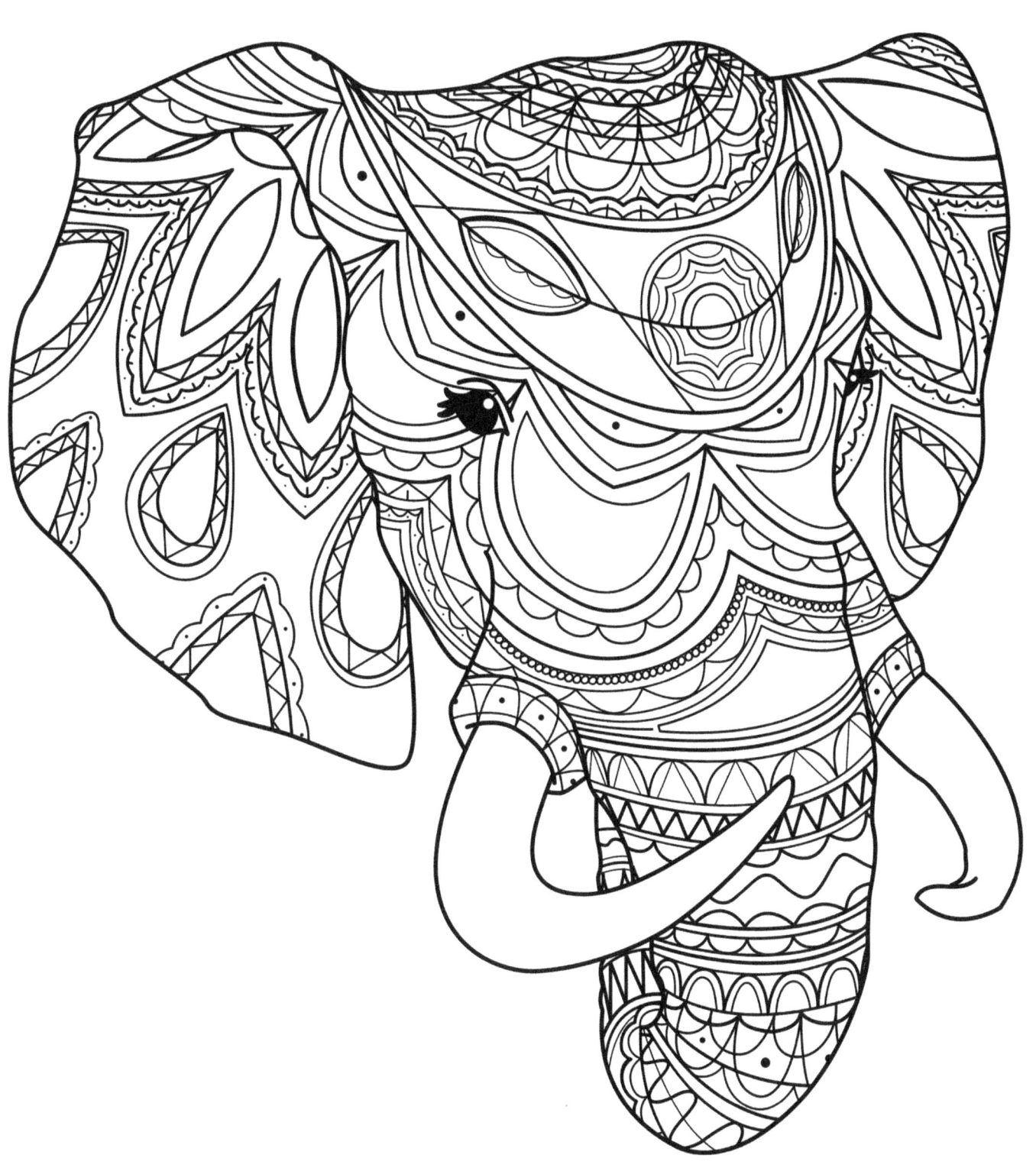

There are always flowers for those who want to see them.

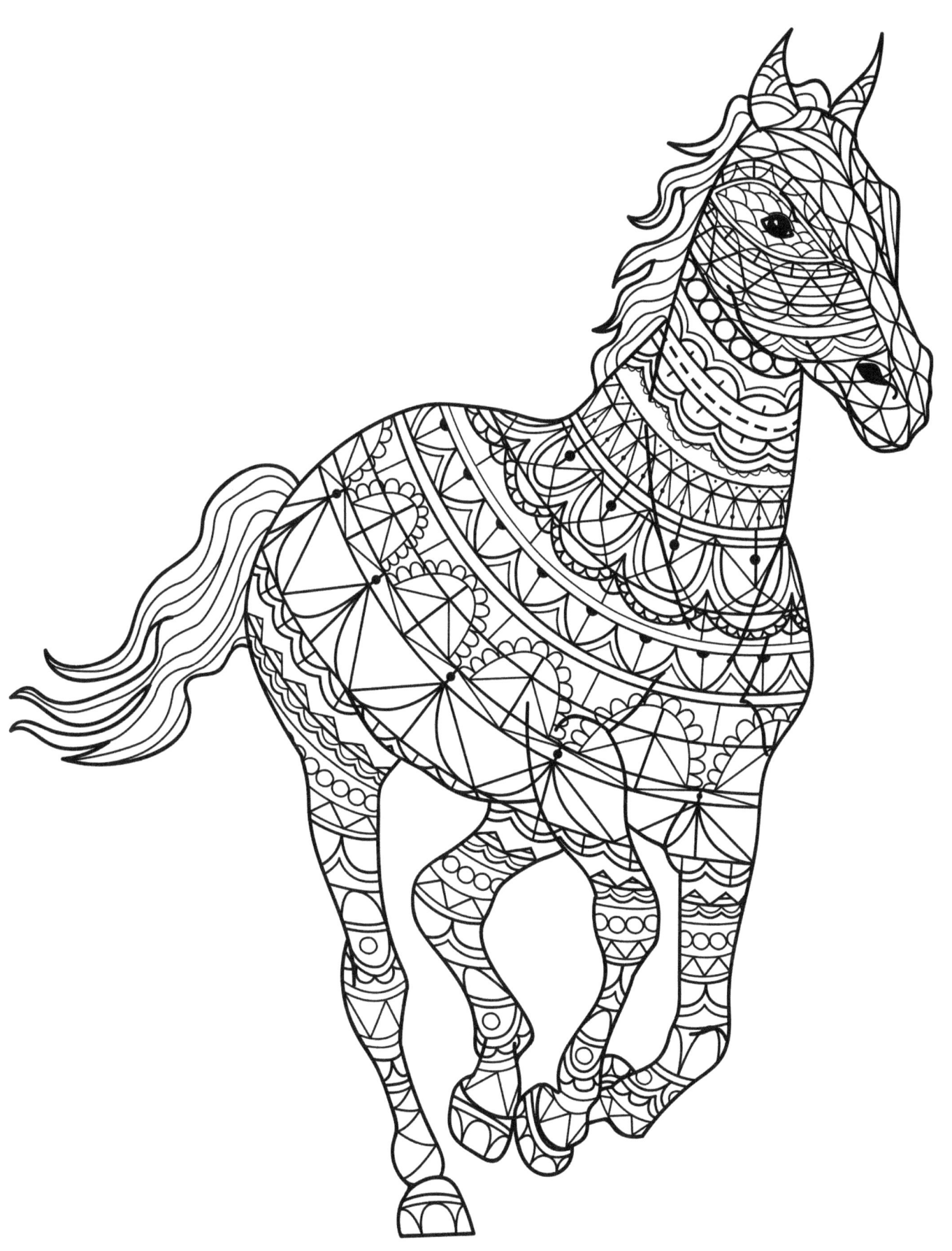

Sunshine is delicious, rain is refreshing, wind braces us up, snow is exhilarating; there is really no such thing as bad weather, only different kinds of good weather.

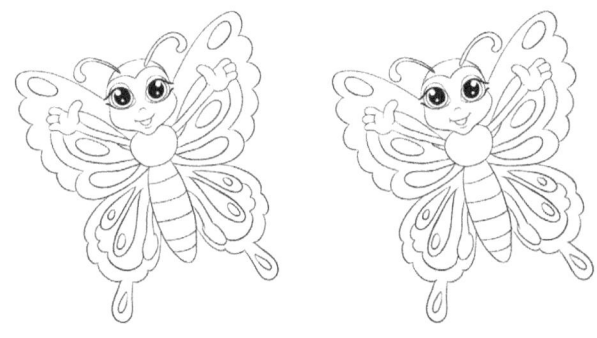

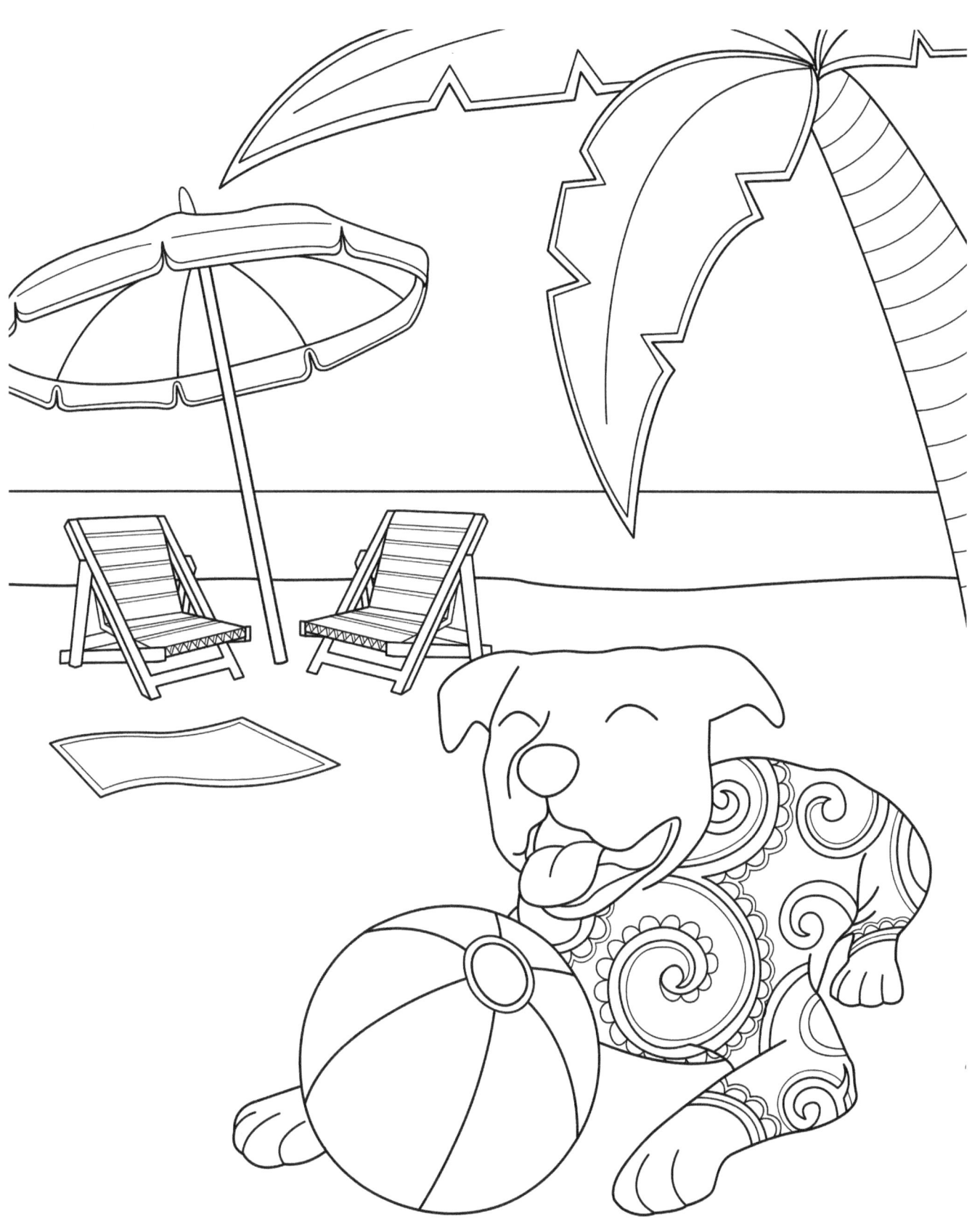

Sunset is still my favorite color, and rainbow is second.

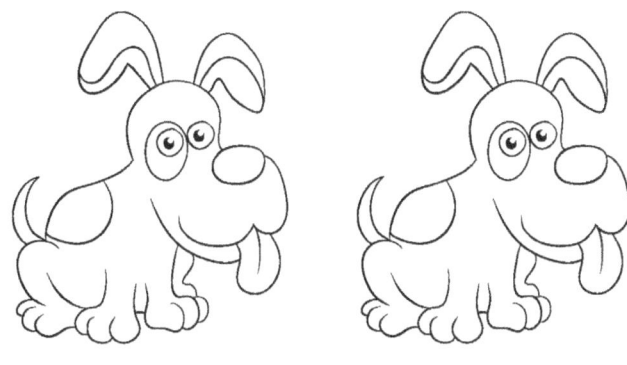

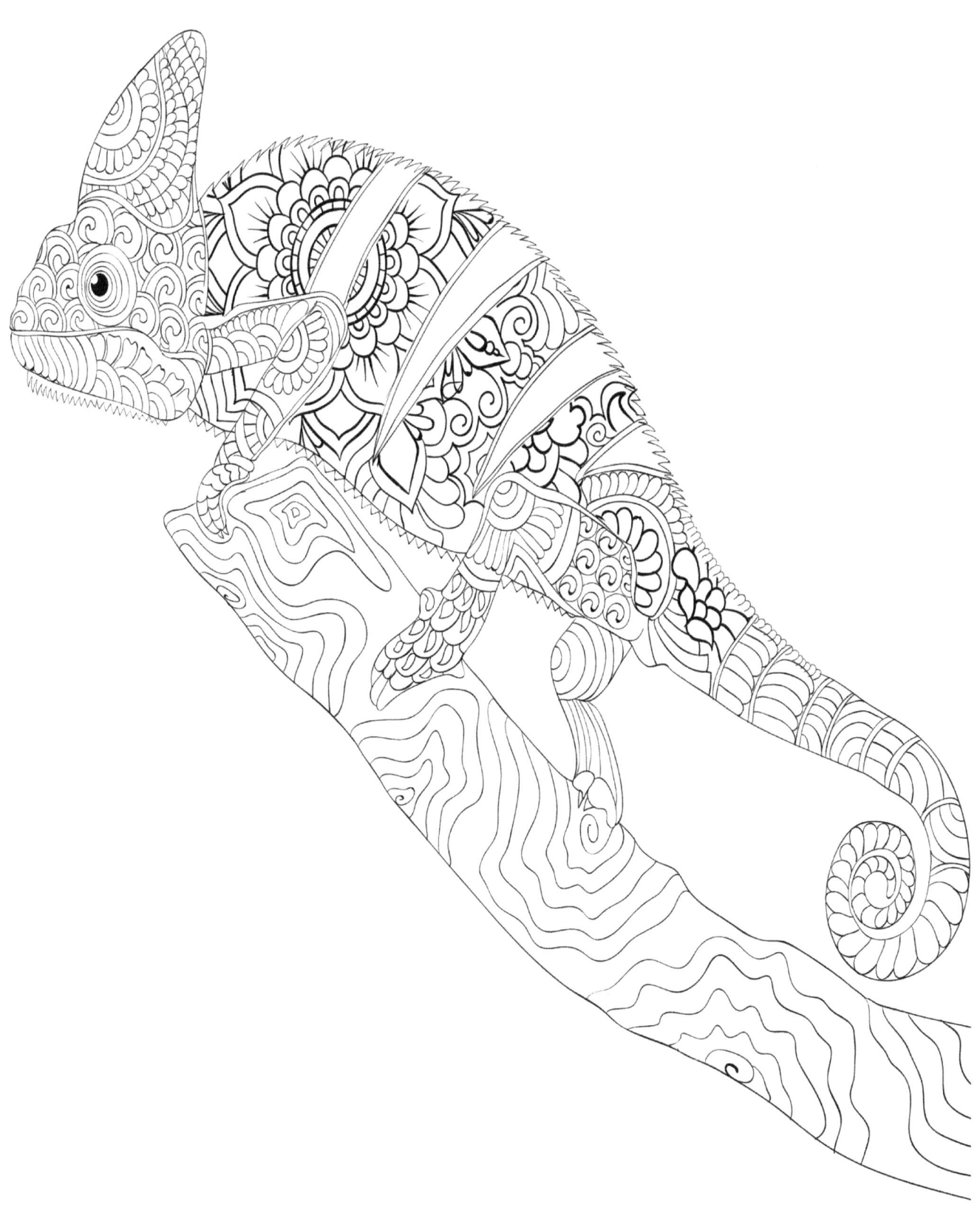

Green is the prime color of the world, and that from which its loveliness arises.

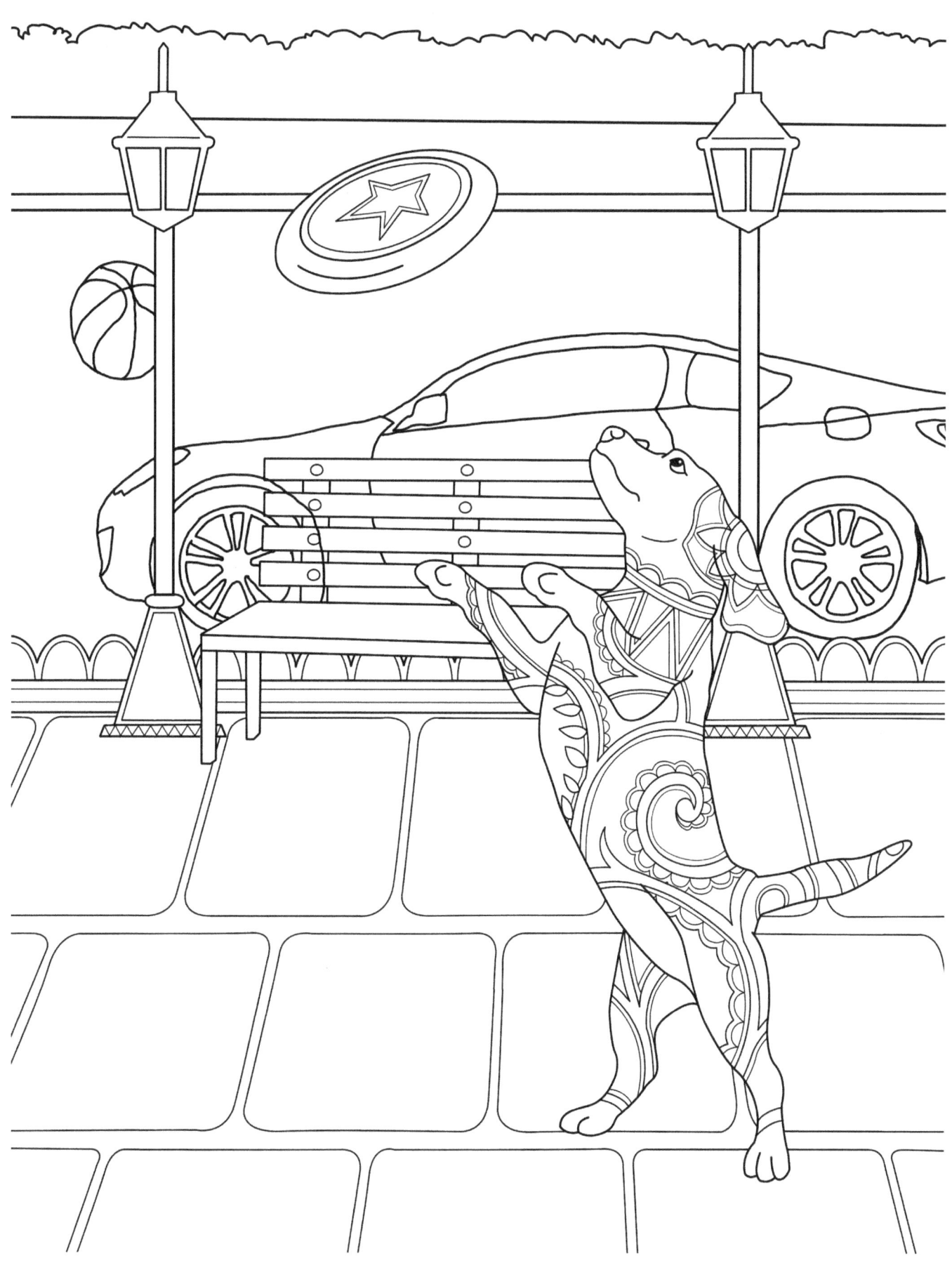

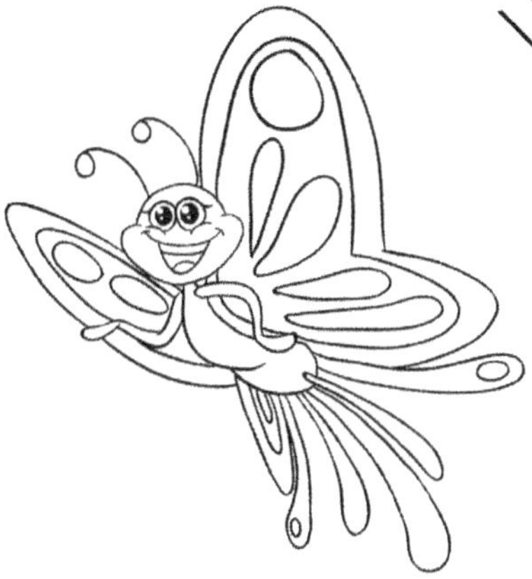

WORK OF THE STARS THAN THE JOURNEY I BELIEVE A LEAF OF GRASS IS NO LESS

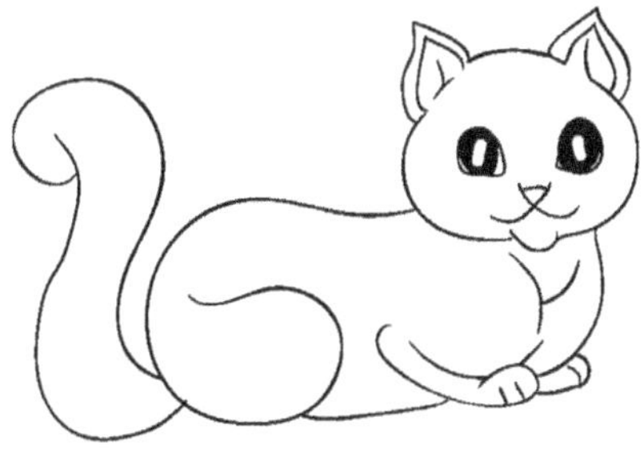

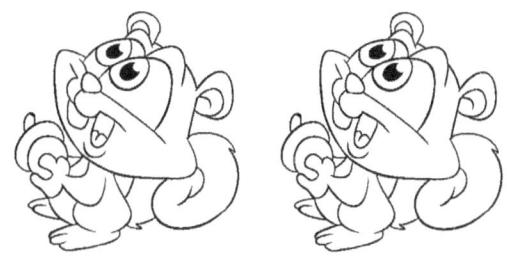

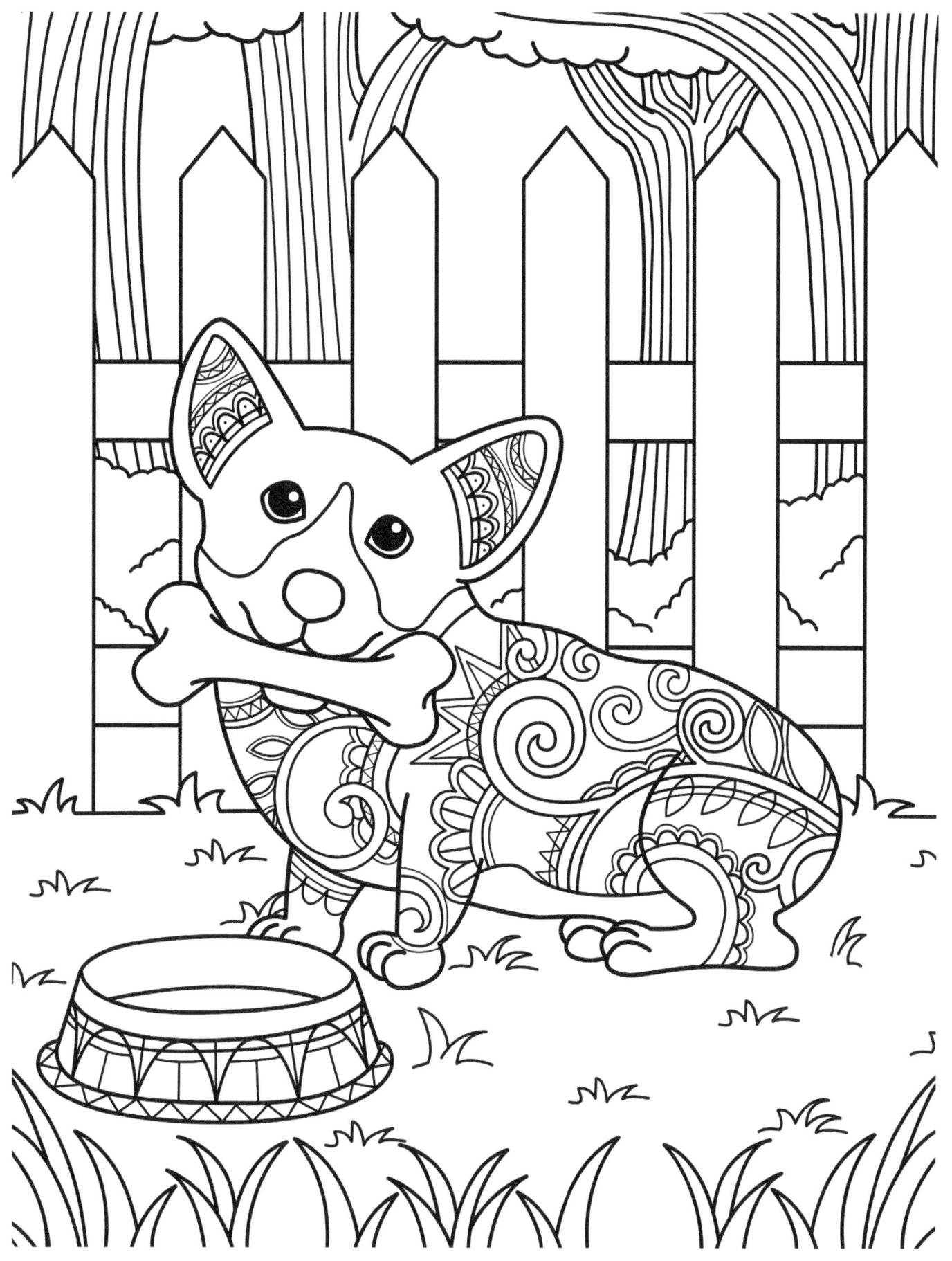

I believe a leaf of grass is no less than the journey-work of the stars.

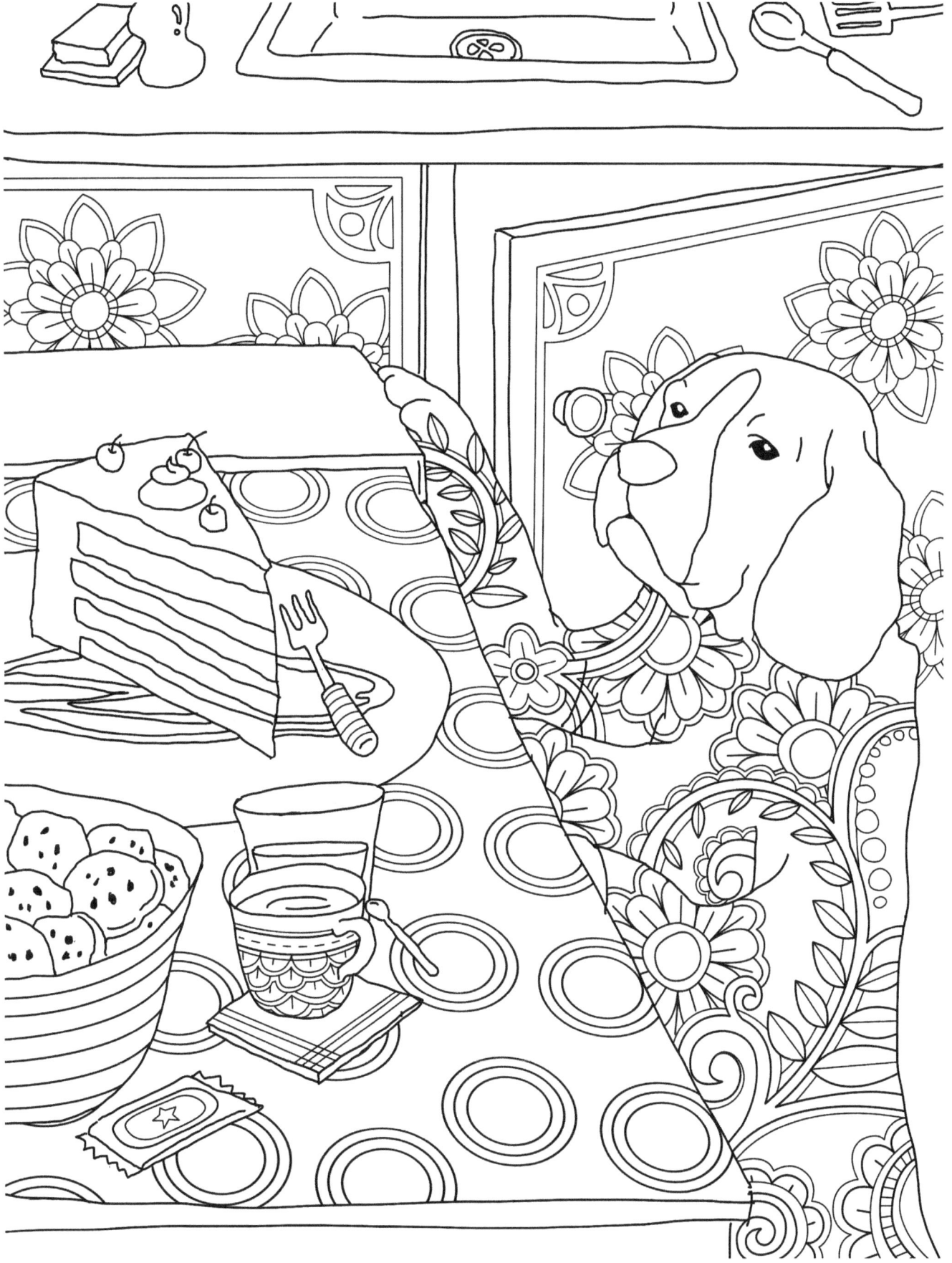

In the depth of winter I finally learned that there was in me an invincible summer.

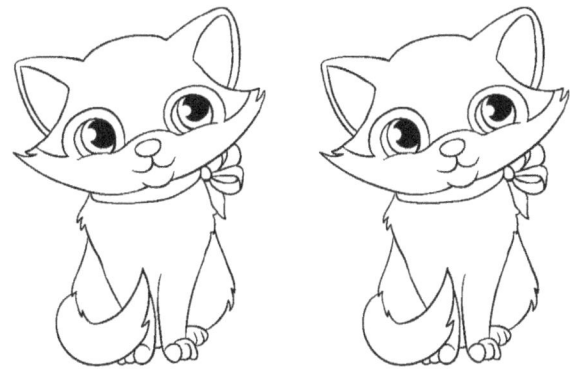

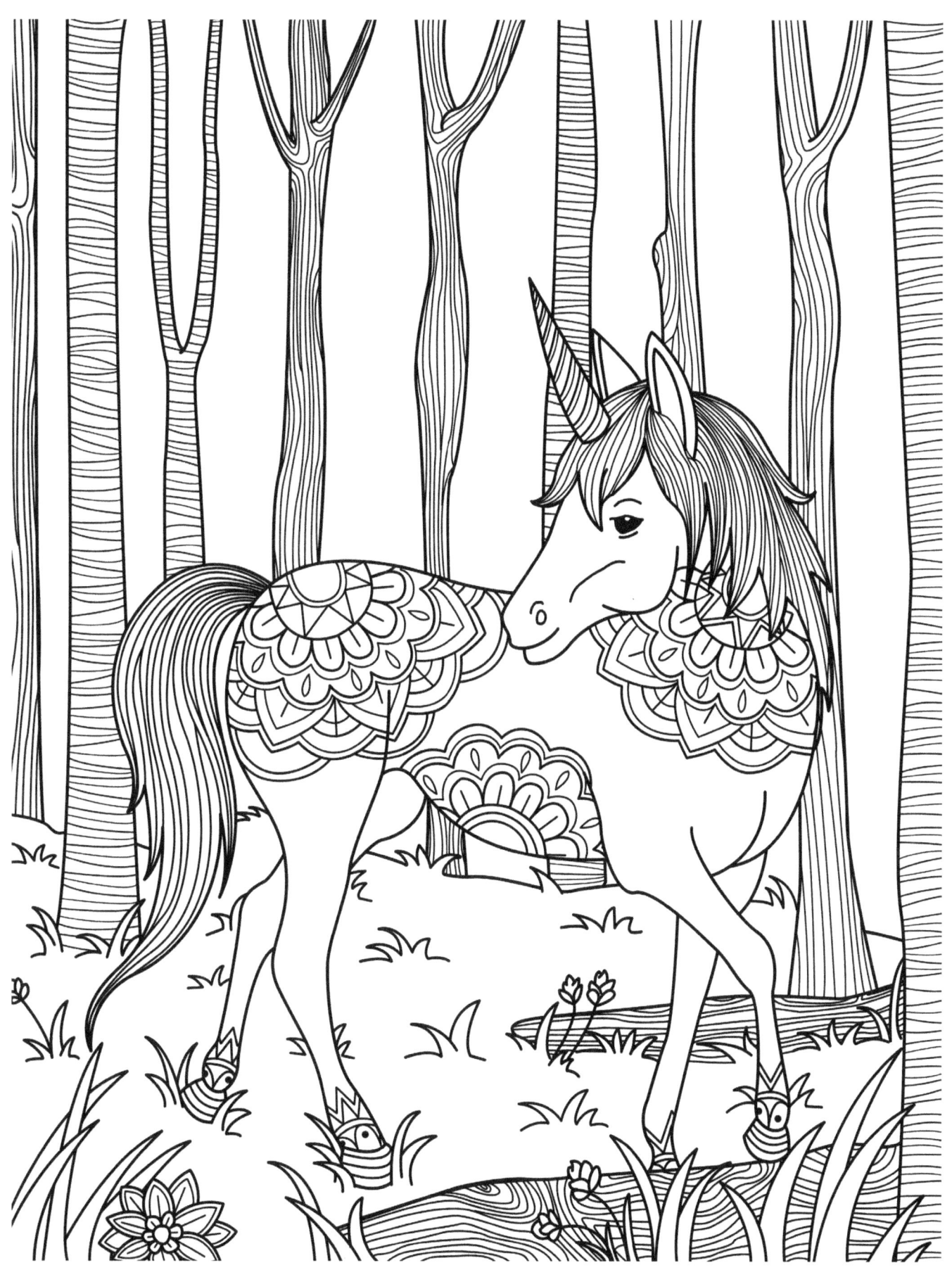

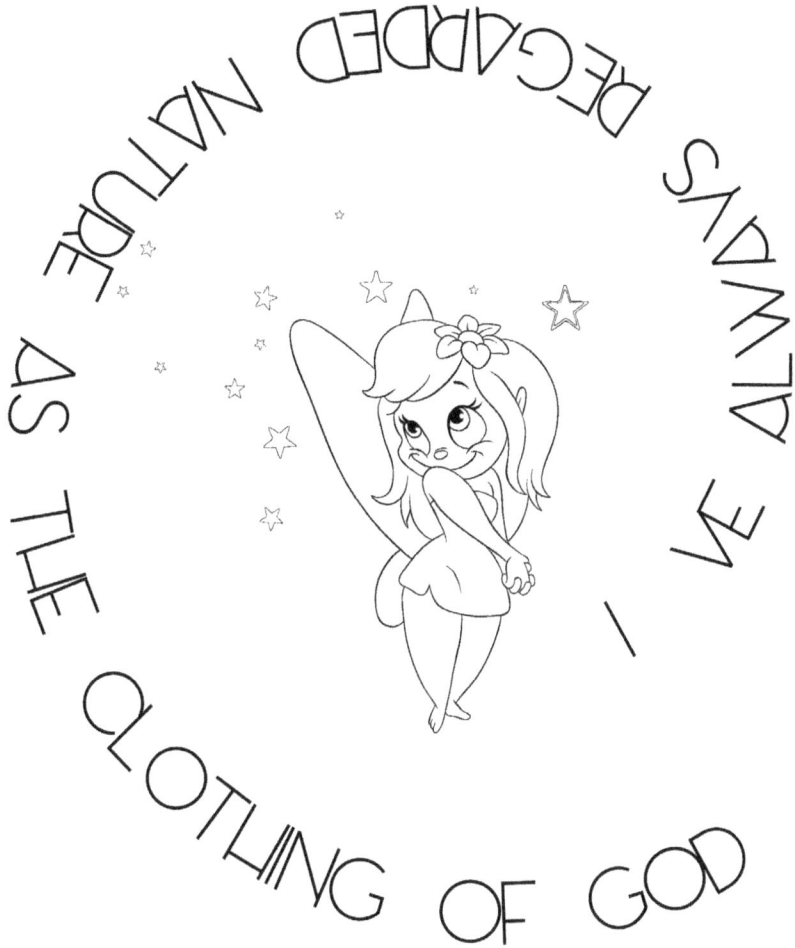

I'VE ALWAYS REGARDED NATURE AS THE CLOTHING OF GOD

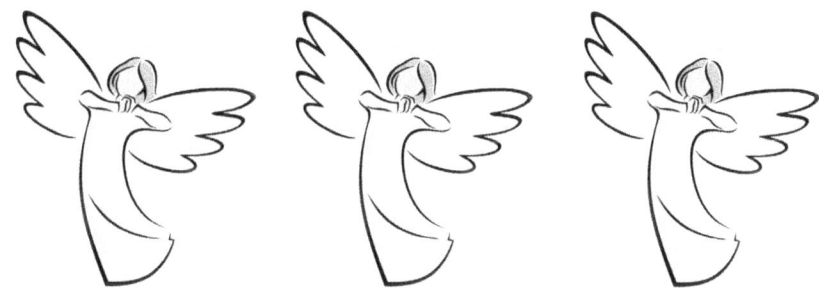

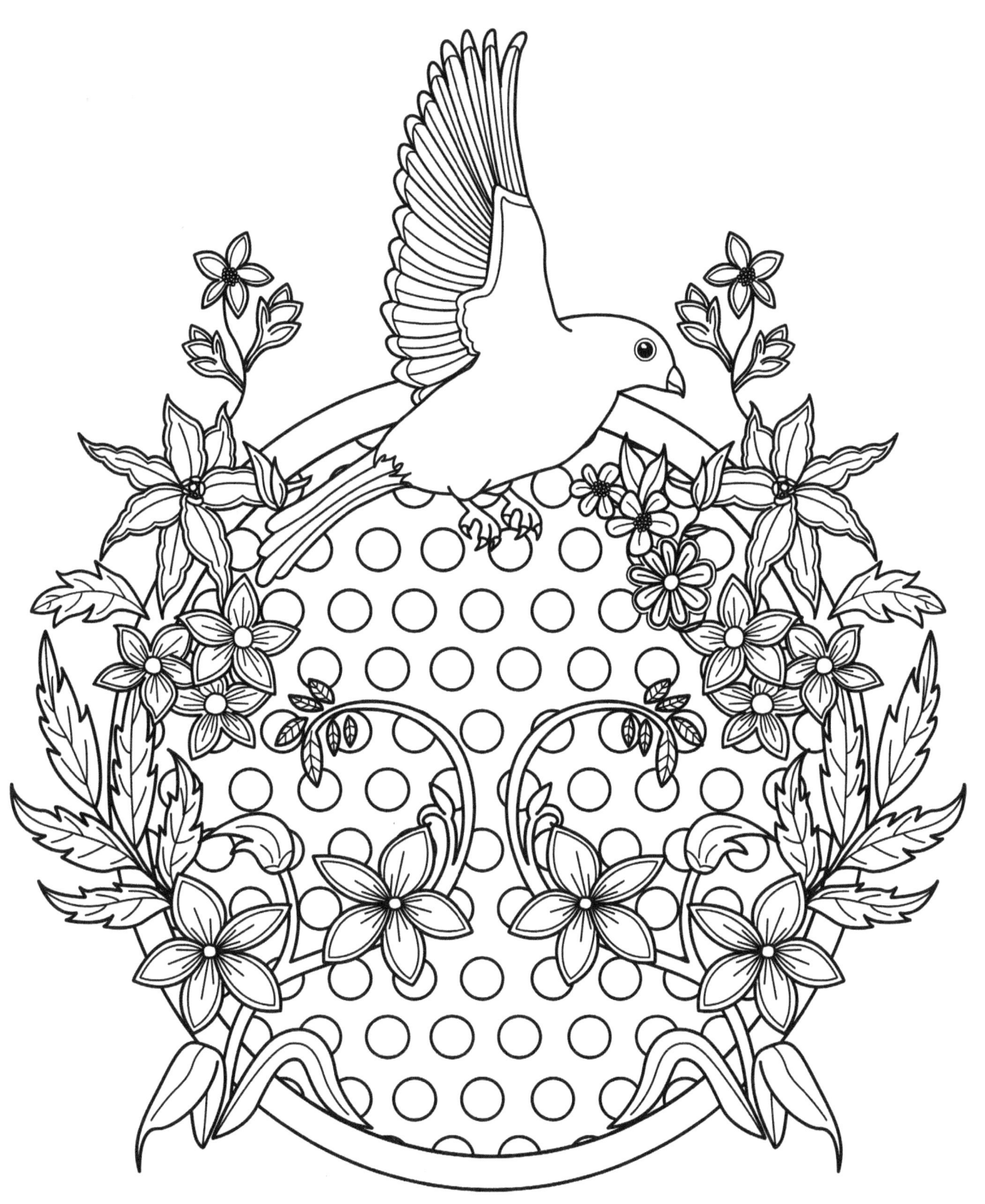

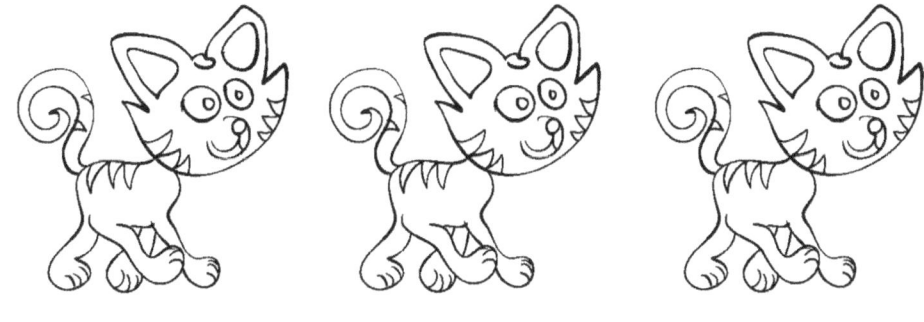

Spring won't let me stay in this house any longer! I must get out and breathe the air deeply again.

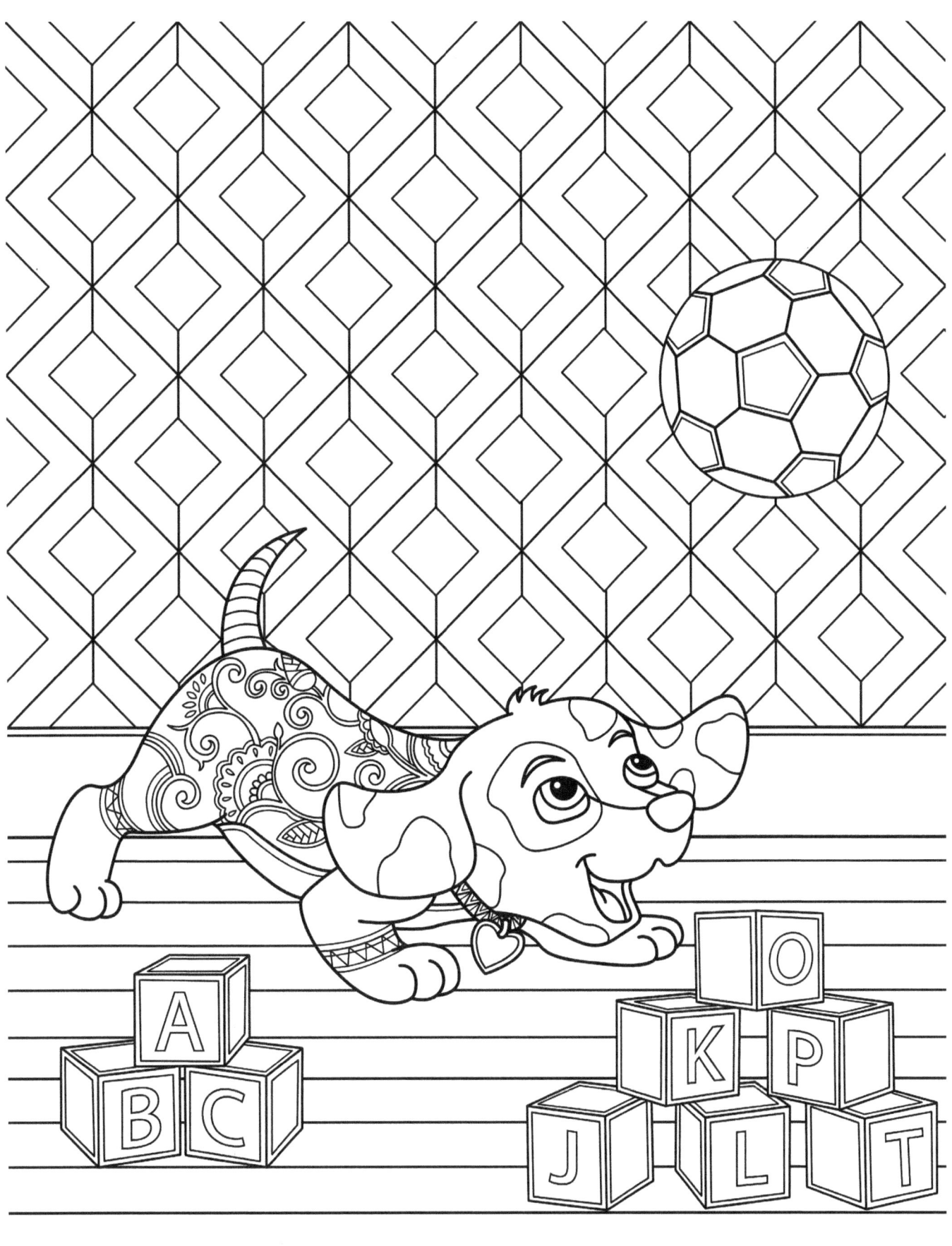

Let the rain kiss you. Let the rain beat upon your head with silver liquid drops. Let the rain sing you a lullaby.

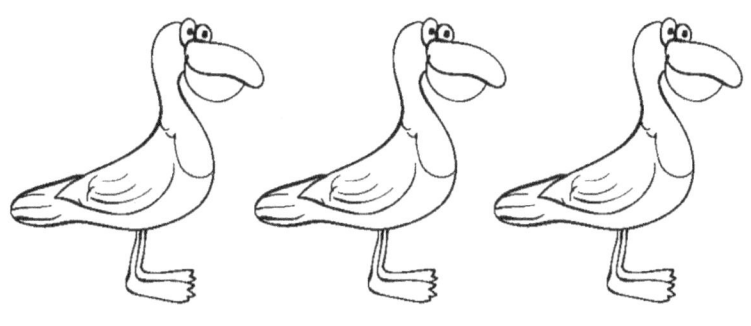

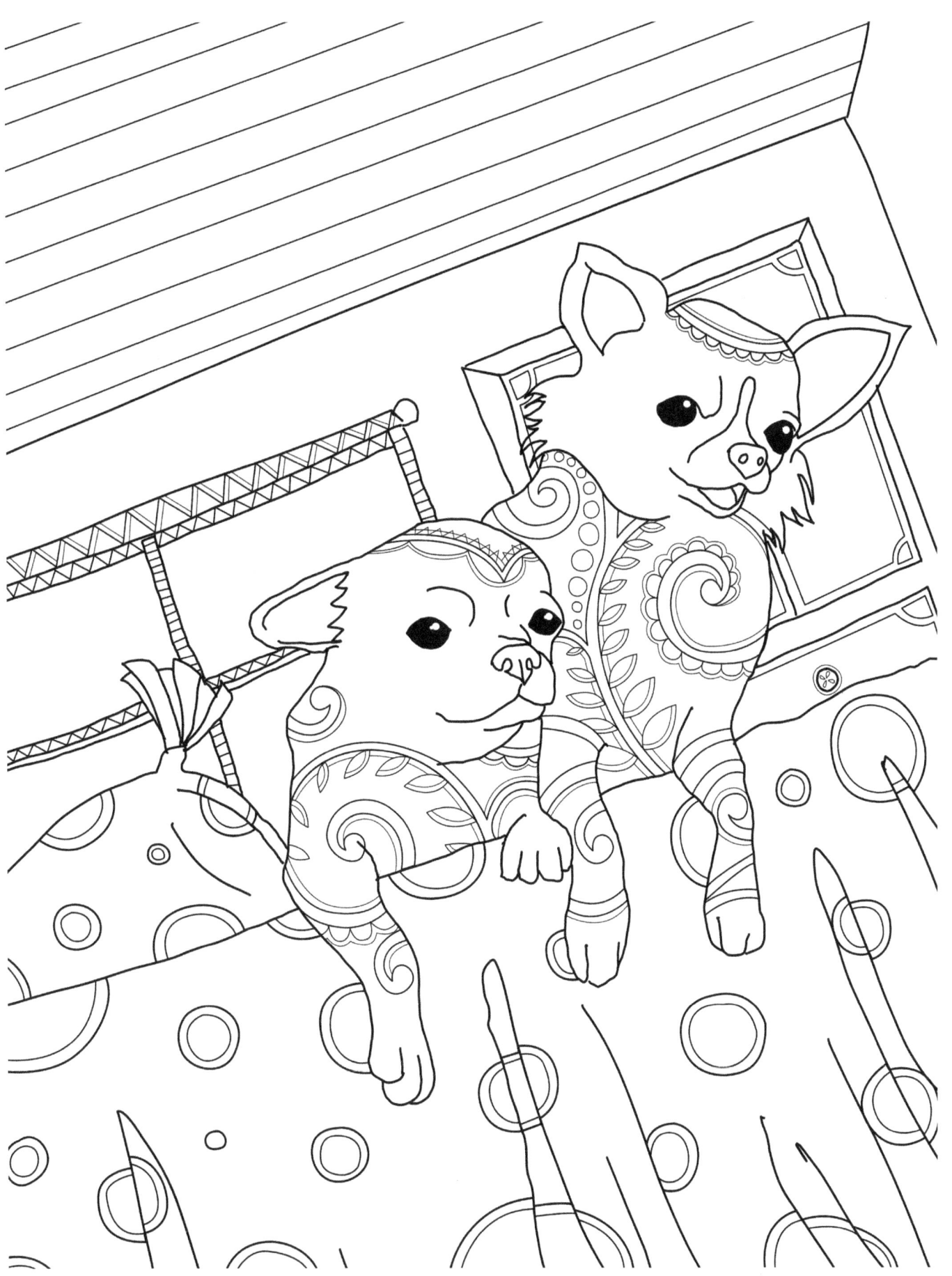

Rain is grace; rain is the sky descending to the earth; without rain, there would be no life.

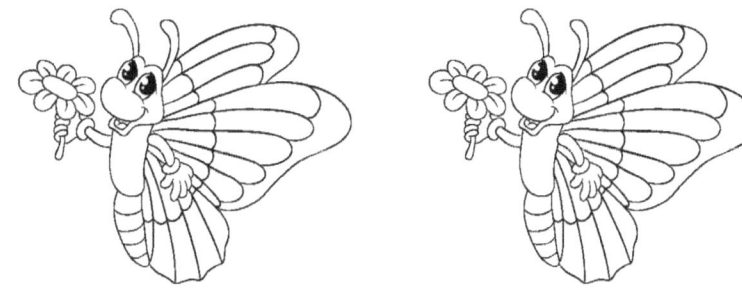

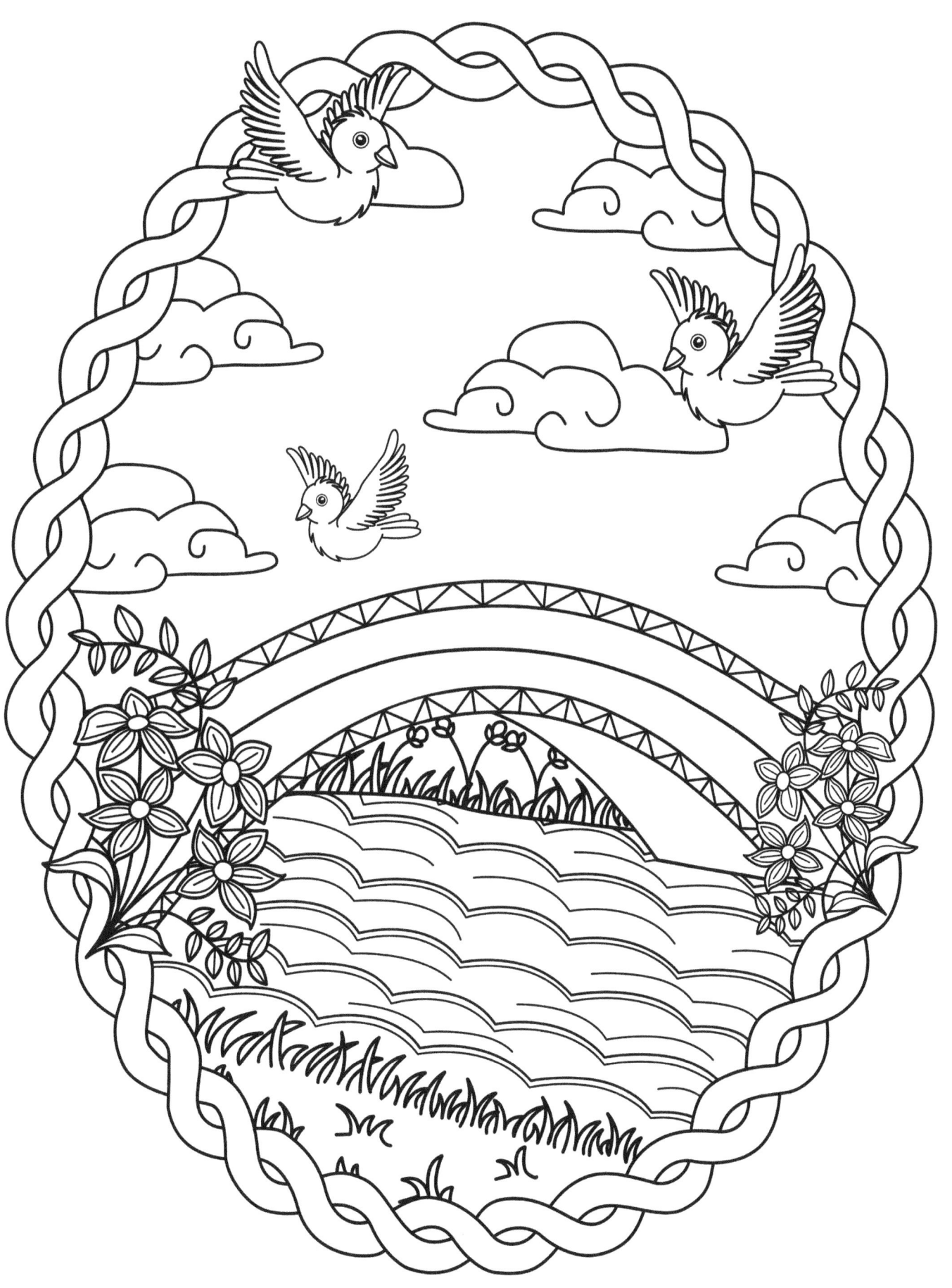

For my part I know nothing with any certainty, but the sight of the stars makes me dream.

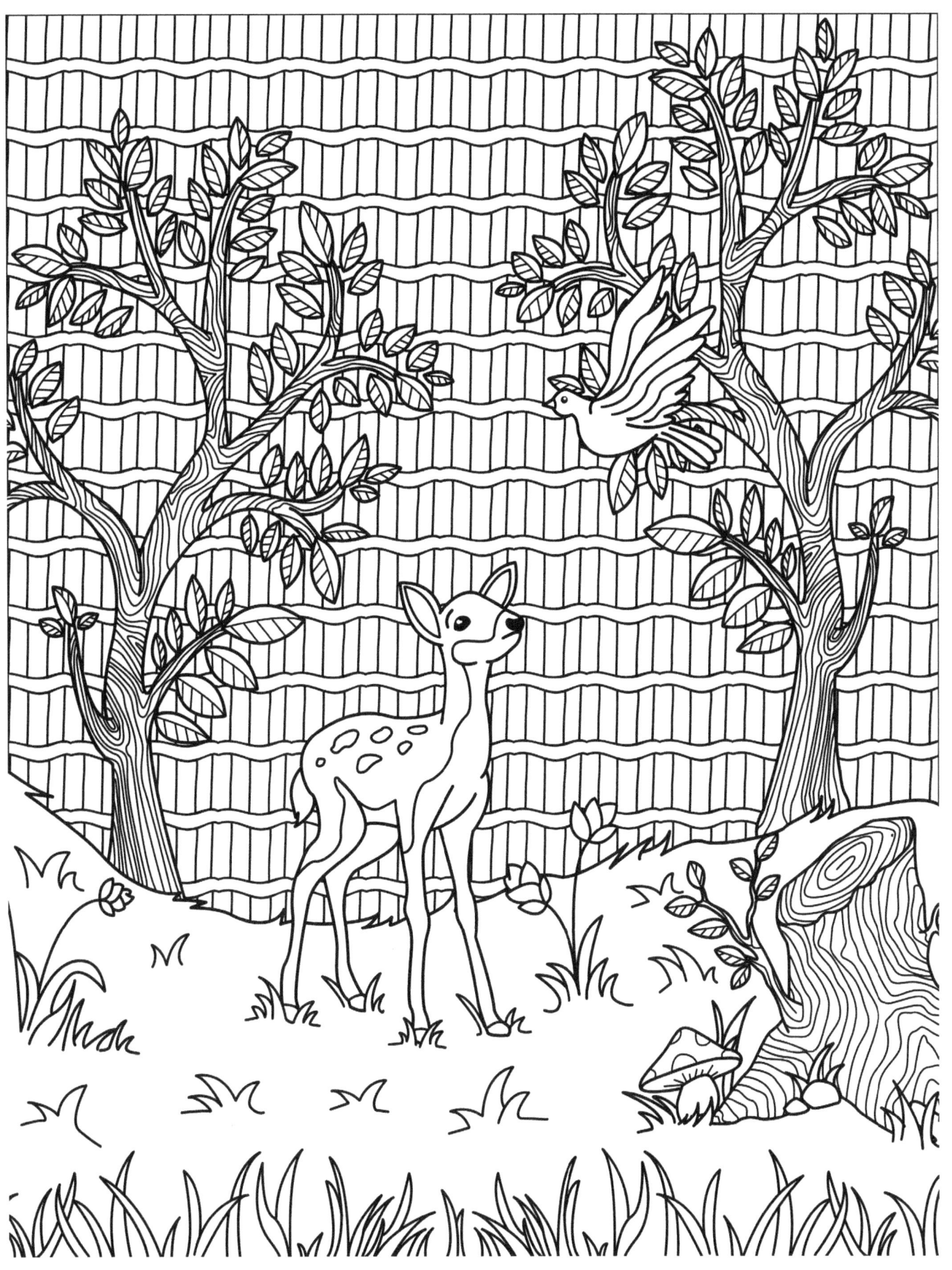

All water has a perfect memory and is forever trying to get back to where it was.

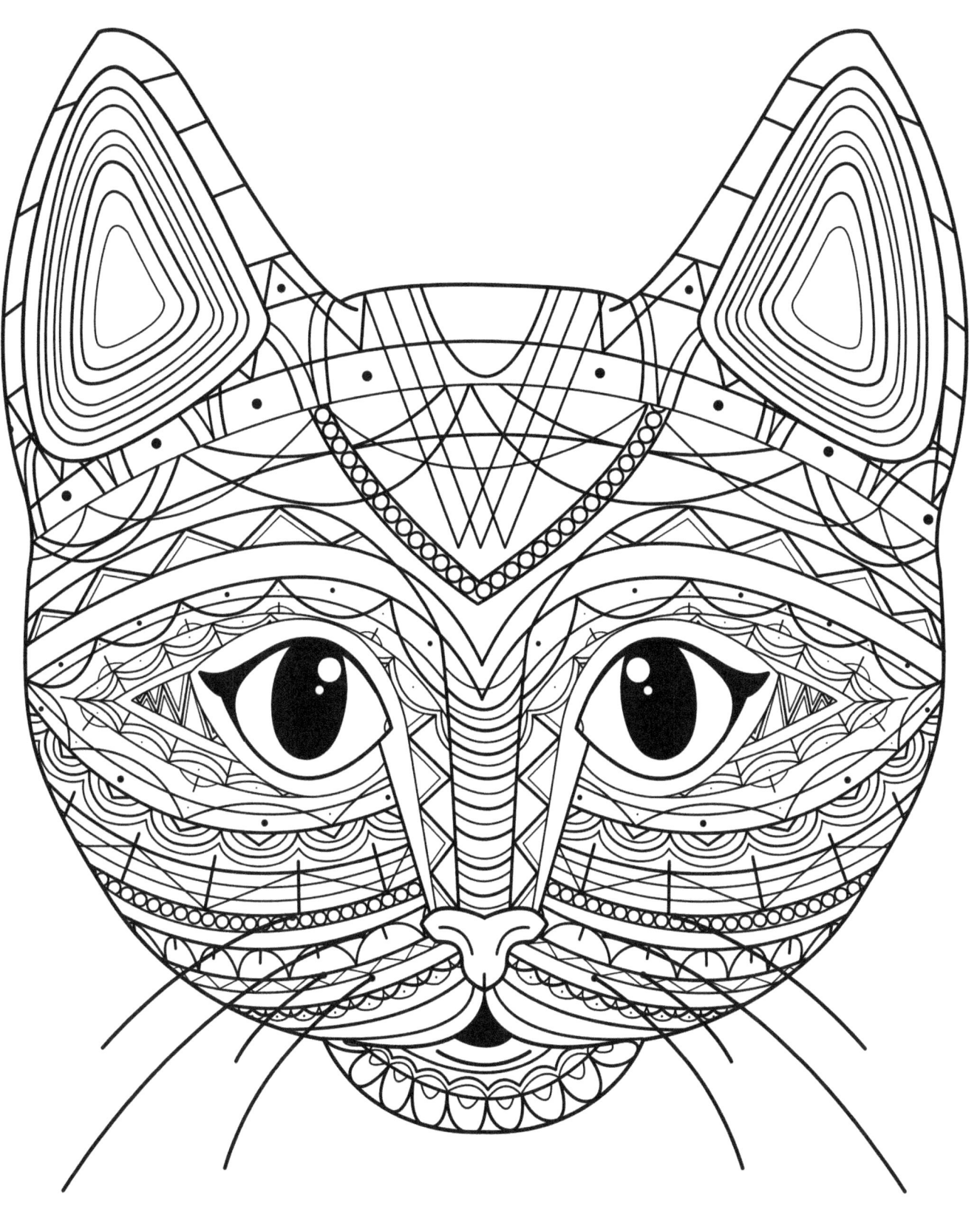

O, wind, if winter comes, can spring be far behind?

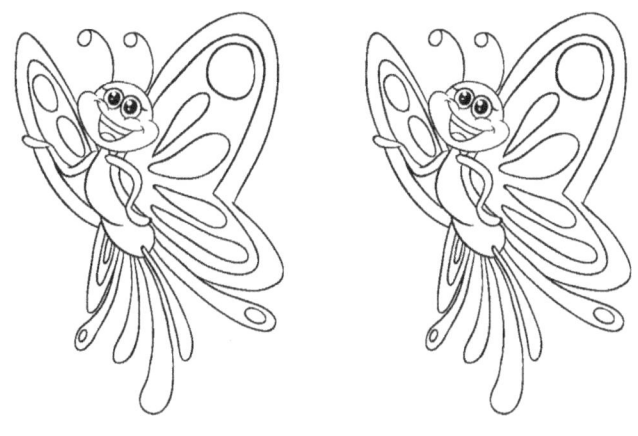

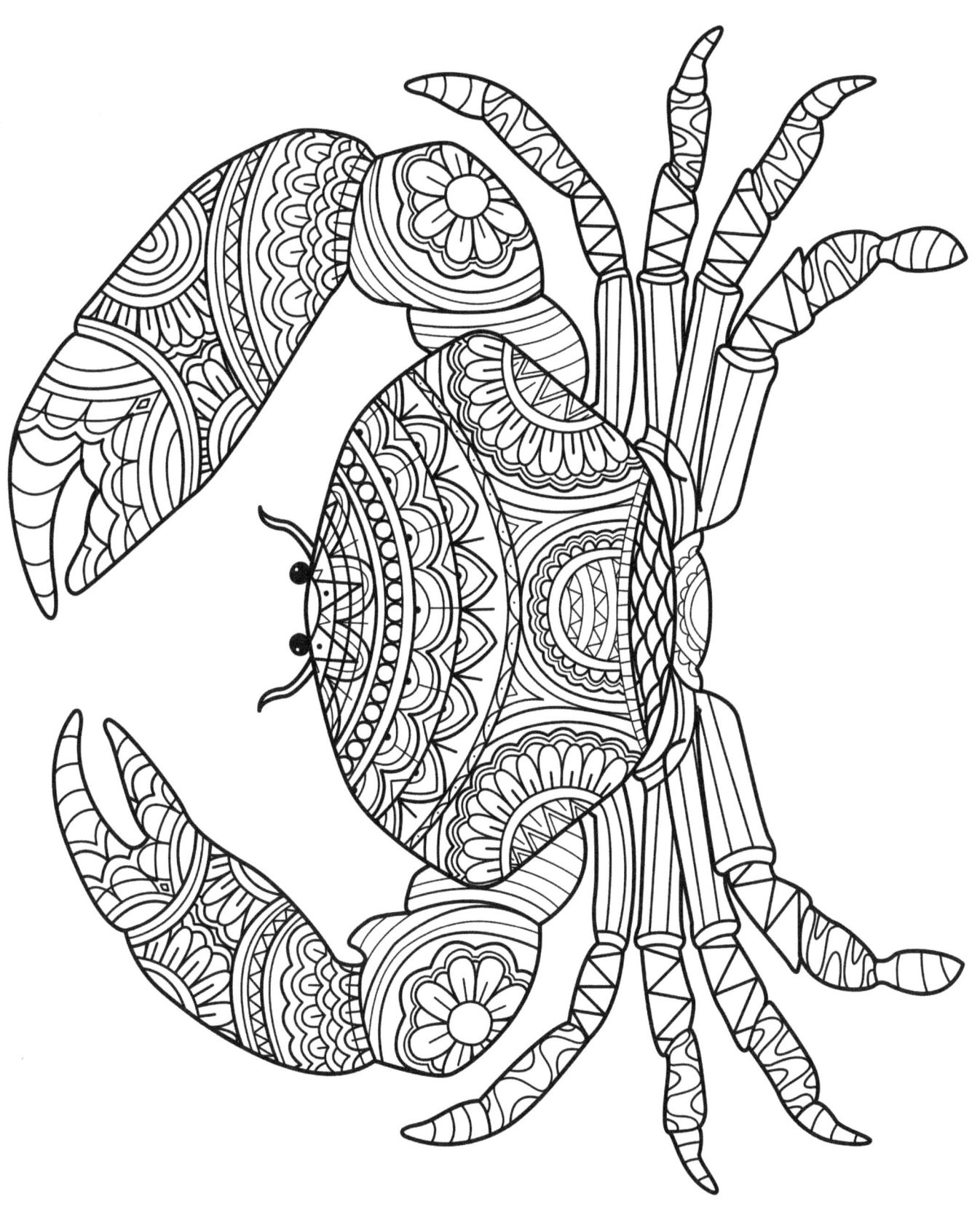

What nature delivers to us is never stale. Because what nature create s has eternity in it.

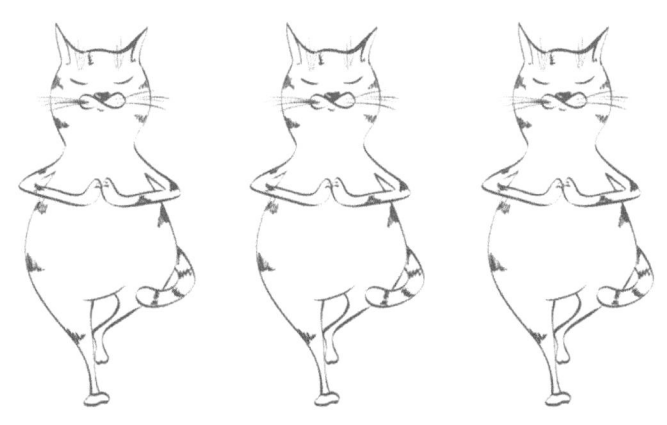

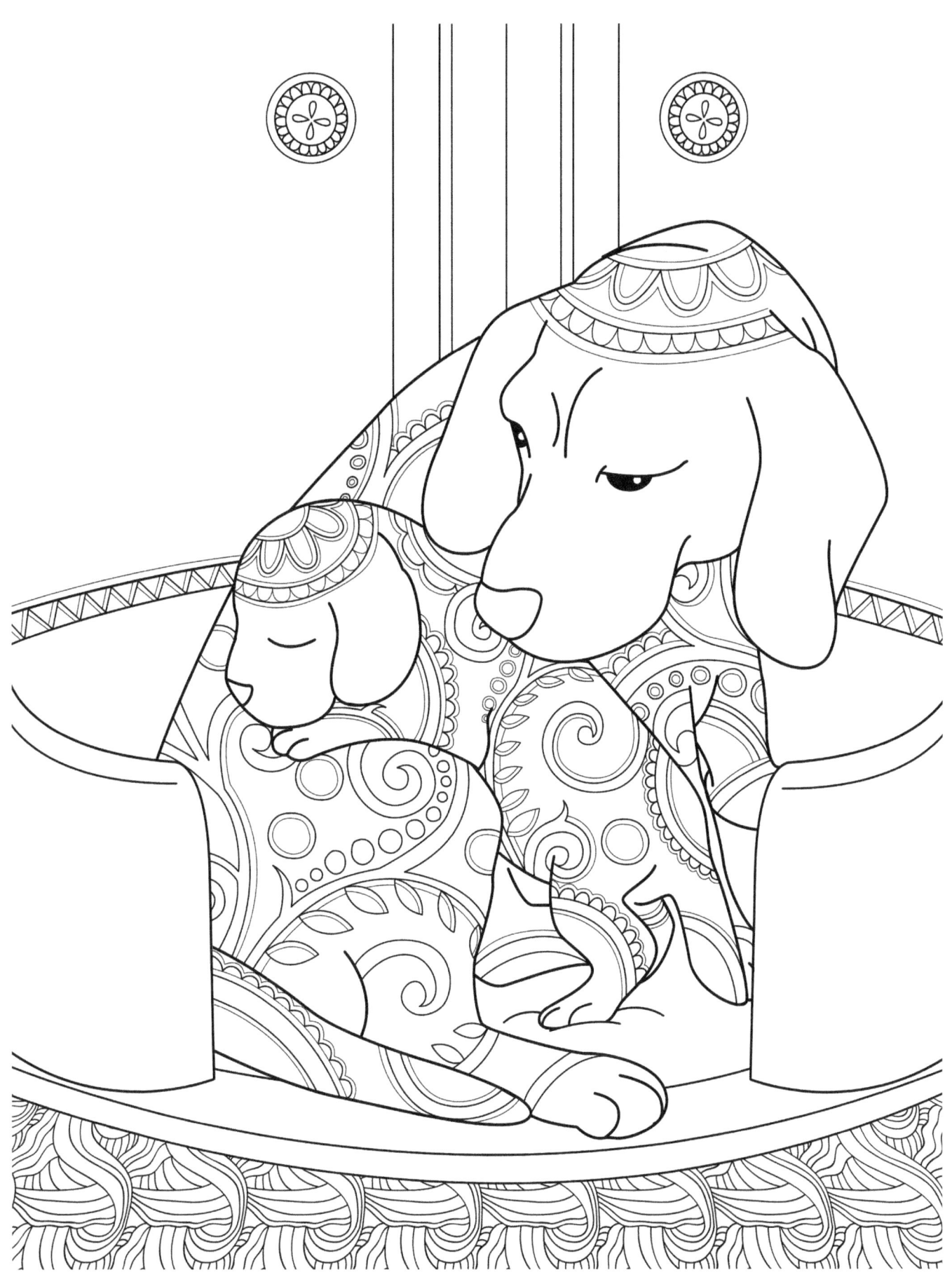

Autumn is a second spring when every leaf is a flower.

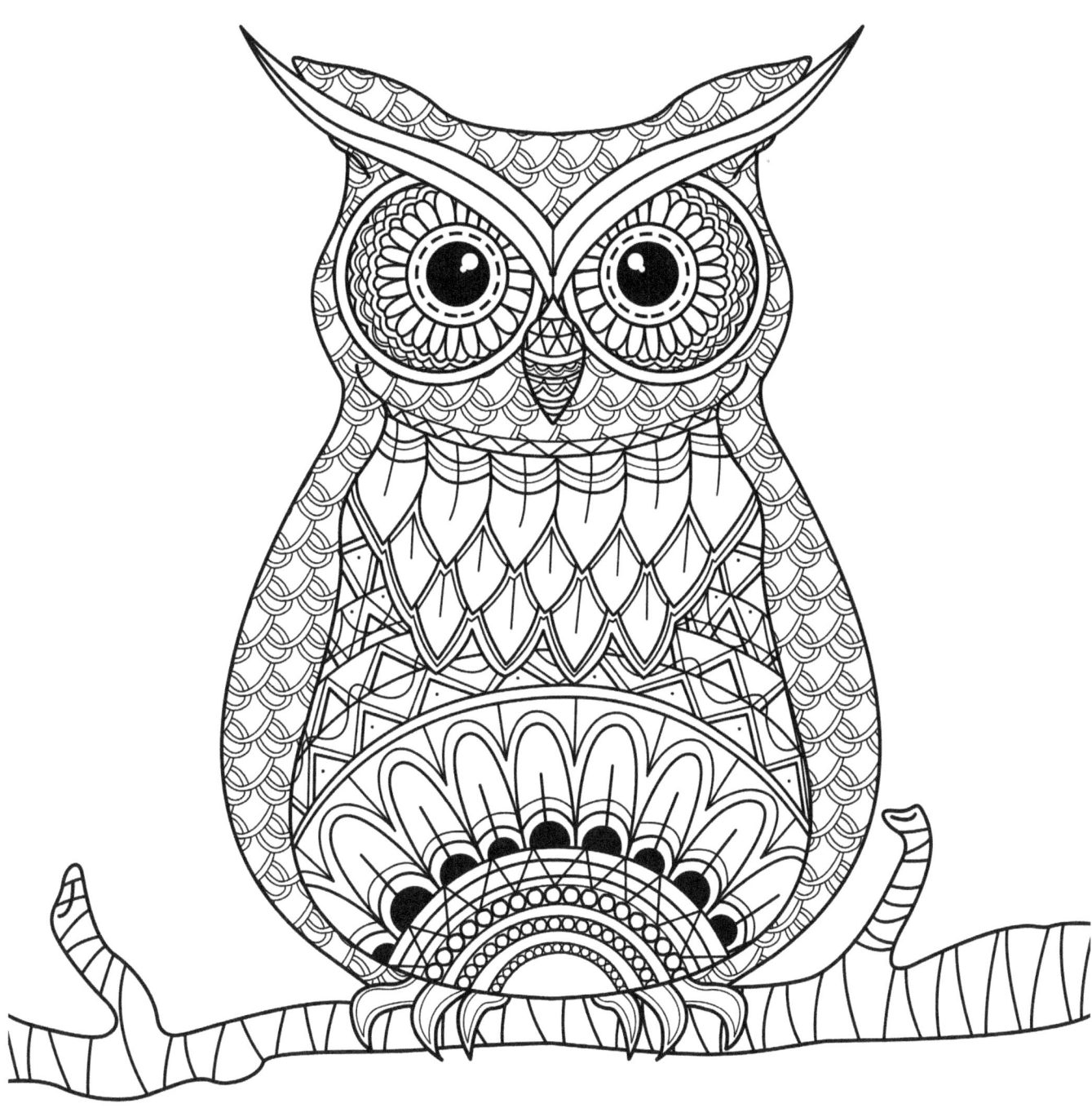

Knowing grass, I can appreciate persistence. Knowing trees, I understand the meaning of patience.

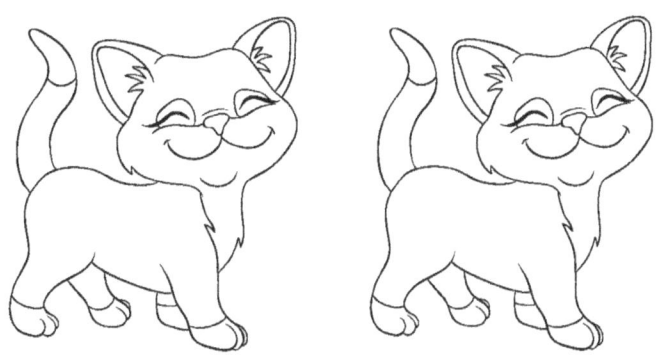

www.ingramcontent.com/pod-product-compliance
Lightning Source LLC
Chambersburg PA
CBHW080624190526
45169CB00009B/3280